$58.70

58-16-01

Quality Middle Schools

Open and Healthy

Wayne K. Hoy
Dennis J. Sabo
in collaboration with
Kevin M. Barnes
John W. Hannum
James D. Hoffman

CORWIN PRESS, INC.
A Sage Publications Company
Thousand Oaks, California

For information:

Corwin Press, Inc.
A Sage Publications Company
2455 Teller Road
Thousand Oaks, California 91320
E-mail: order@corwin.sagepub.com

SAGE Publications Ltd.
6 Bonhill Street
London EC2A 4PU
United Kingdom

SAGE Publications India Pvt. Ltd.
M-32 Market
Greater Kailash I
New Delhi 110 048 India

Printed in the United States of America

Library of Congress Cataloging-in-Publication Data

Hoy, Wayne K.
    Quality middle schools: Open and healthy/By Wayne K. Hoy, Dennis J. Sabo;
  in collaboration with Kevin M. Barnes, John W. Hannum, James D. Hoffman.
        p. cm.
    Includes bibliographical references and index.
    ISBN 0-8039-6420-X (cloth: acid-free paper).—ISBN 0-8039-6421-8
  (pbk.: acid-free paper)
      1. Middle schools—United States. 2. School environment—United States.
  3. School management and organization—United States. I. Sabo, Dennis J.
  II. Barnes, Kevin M. III. Hannum, John W. IV. Hoffman, James D., 1954–
  V. Title.
    LB1623.5.H69 1997
    373.236—dc21   97-4883

This book is printed on acid-free paper.

98 99 00 01 02 03 10 9 8 7 6 5 4 3 2 1

Production Editor: Sherrise M. Purdum
Production Assistant: Denise Santoyo
Editorial Assistant: Kristen L. Gibson
Typesetter/Designer: Marion Warren
Cover Designer: Marcia M. Rosenburg
Print Buyer: Anna Chin

CONTENTS

Prior Books by Wayne K. Hoy and Others
on Open and Healthy Schools
(Note: Some content and instruments overlap in these publications)

Open Schools/Healthy Schools: Measuring Organizational Climate (1991) by Wayne K. Hoy, C. John Tarter, and Robert B. Kottkamp

The Road to Open and Healthy Schools: A Handbook for Change, Middle and Secondary School Edition (1997a) by Wayne K. Hoy and C. John Tarter

The Road to Open and Health Schools: A Handbook for Change, Elementary and Middle School Edition (1997b) by Wayne K. Hoy and C. John Tarter

PREFACE

Quality Middle Schools: Open and Healthy is the culmination of nearly two decades of research and development. It is the fourth book in a series (Hoy, Tarter, & Kottkamp, 1991; Hoy & Tarter, 1997a, 1997b) and brings our study of school climate to a natural conclusion. The focus of this work is strictly on the middle school. Our purpose is twofold: to provide educational researchers with a set of reliable and valid measures to study the nature of the middle schools, and to provide practitioners with a set of tools to evaluate their school climate with an aim toward organizational improvement.

We use personality and health metaphors to explore the organizational climates of schools. The openness of a school climate is measured by the Organizational Climate Description Questionnaire (Revised) for Middle Schools (OCDQ-RM) and the health of school climate is determined by the Organizational Health Inventory for Middle Schools (OHI-M). The conceptual foundations for these instruments as well as their technical details are described for researchers and scholars interested in using the frameworks and instruments in their own work. In addition, a summary of basic research demonstrates the utility of the measures in studying school outcomes. For practitioners, who may be less interested in the technical properties, there are step-by-step directions for administering, scoring, and interpreting the measures. For graduate students, we have presented a rough outline of a research agenda for the middle school that will provide many doctoral students with research projects for years to come.

The book will be read differently by researchers, practitioners, and graduate students. Researchers will want to read carefully the first four chapters, which provide an overview of the frameworks, technical details of the instruments, and research findings; then browse the last chapter, which provides copies of the instruments and scoring directions. Practitioners will be interested in the overview and discussion of quality in the first chapter and the hands-on information necessary to use the climate measures in the last chapter. We recommend that practitioners also browse Chapters 2, 3, and 4 to get a sense of the technical details of the instrument and the research findings. To make for a user-friendly survey of the research findings, we have *italicized* the conclusions in Chapter 4 so that by simply perusing the *italicized* print, the reader can get a quick sense of the research findings. Graduate students should read every word with a critical and open mind.

This work has involved a large number of people. The impetus for the original project came in a theory and research course that I taught in 1980 at Rutgers University as my students and I read and discussed the conceptual and empirical work of Andrew Halpin and Matthew Miles. The first stage of our research focused on elementary and secondary schools (Hoy, Tarter, & Kottkamp, 1991). *Quality Middle Schools: Open and Healthy* describes the last phase of the research project. The team for the current investigation consisted of Kevin M. Barnes, James D. Hoffman, John W. Hannum, and Dennis J. Sabo.

We are saddened by the tragic death of Dennis Sabo, our friend, colleague, and comrade in work, who died in the ValuJet crash in the Everglades in May 1996. His loss was a shock. This project would not have been possible without his interest, work, and commitment. Dennis was a rare combination of scholar and practitioner, one who enriched the lives of his colleagues and students. His legacy lives on through the many lives he touched, and we dedicate *Quality Middle Schools: Open and Healthy* to Dennis and his life and memory.

A few other colleagues should be recognized. Thank you to Patrick Forsyth, Cecil Miskel, and I. Phillip Young, who read parts of the manuscript and made many useful suggestions. My friend and colleague, John Tarter, also provided a critical eye, and most of the ideas in the last chapter we developed jointly in earlier projects. A special thanks goes to Megan Tschannen-Moran who made substantial editorial contributions to the clarity of the presentations. She is also responsible for the art work, graphs, and charts. We also thank Wayne K. Hoy, II of Advanced Software Products for writing a PC scoring program for Windows, which is now available through Arlington Writers, 2548 Onandaga Drive, Columbus, Ohio 43221. The program makes it simple to score and interpret the climate measures using a personal computer. Finally, I would be remiss if I did not acknowledge the influence of my wife, Anita Woolfolk Hoy, who has a ready ear for my latest ideas and prose. She always provides a gentle criticism that improves both my thinking and writing. It is a better book because of the help I received from all of my colleagues, but I accept responsibility for any mistakes.

We believe that there is sufficient skill and talent in the schools for the principal and teachers to work collaboratively to make their school a better place. All they need is the time, the desire, and the means. School boards can contribute the time; administrators can furnish the leadership, and this book delivers the means. We encourage all interested researchers and practitioners to use our work. There is no fee; just copy the instruments and use them. We ask only that you share your results with us so that we can refine the measures, develop more comprehensive norms, and add to the body of knowledge about school climate and change. We have supplied a simple form in the appendix to gather such information. Address all correspondence to Professor Wayne K. Hoy, College of Education, 29 West Woodruff Avenue, Ohio State University, Columbus, Ohio, 43210.

WKH
Naples, Florida

ABOUT THE AUTHORS

Wayne K. Hoy, former Chair of the Department of Educational Administration, Associate Dean of Academic Affairs, and Distinguished Professor at Rutgers University, is the Novice Fawcett Chair in Educational Administration at Ohio State University. He received his B.A. from Lock Haven State College in 1959 and his D.Ed. from Pennsylvania State University in 1965. His primary research interests are theory and research in administration, the sociology of organizations, and the social psychology of administration. In 1973, he received the Lindback Foundation Award for Distinguished Teaching from Rutgers University; in 1987, he was given the Alumni Award for Professional Research from the Graduate School of Education; in 1991, he received the Excellence in Education Award from Pennsylvania State University; and in 1992, he was given the Meritorious Research Award from the Eastern Educational Research Association. He currently serves on the editorial boards of *Educational Administration Quarterly, Journal of Educational Administration, McGill Journal of Education,* and the *Journal of Research and Development* *in Education.* He has written more than a hundred books, articles, chapters, and papers.

Dennis J. Sabo, who was the principal of Bordentown High School and then Manville High School, had a long and distinguished career as an educator in the public schools of New Jersey before becoming a professor of educational administration at Auburn University. He received his B.S. and M.S. from Trenton State College and his Ed.D. from Rutgers University in 1993. He published his research and scholarship in a wide array of journals including the *Journal of Educational Administration, Planning and Changing, Research in Middle-Level Education Quarterly,* and the *Journal of School Leadership.* His career was brought to a sudden and tragic end in May 1996 when the Valu-Jet on which he was a passenger crashed in the Everglades.

ABOUT THE
COLLABORATORS

Kevin M. Barnes (Ed.D., Rutgers University, 1994) is the principal of Wilson Elementary School, West Caldwell, New Jersey. He has been an administrator at the elementary and middle school levels; he was the vice-principal of Ryerson Middle School, Ringwood, New Jersey, when the research for this book was conducted. He is the coauthor of articles that have appeared in *Research in Middle-Level Education Quarterly, Journal of School Leadership*, and research presented at the American Educational Research Association Convention. His research interests include school climate, shared decision making, and trust in organizations.

John W. Hannum (Ed.D., Rutgers University, 1994) is principal of Newton High School, Newton, New Jersey. He was principal of Halsted Middle School in Newton when the research for this book was completed. An adjunct professor at Jersey City State College and Rutgers University, he has made presentations on school climate to a number of professional groups including the American Education-al Research Association and the New Jersey Principals and Super-visors Association. He is coauthor of an article that appeared in *Educational Administration Quarterly*. His research interests include school climate and organizational health, especially as they relate to student achievement.

James D. Hoffman's career has encompassed work as a teacher and administrator in elementary and secondary schools, but the major focus has been his work as a principal and assistant principal on the middle level. His publications on the topic of middle schools have appeared in the *Journal of Educational Administration* and *Journal of School Leadership*. He is a graduate of the College of New Jersey (B.A.) and Rutgers University (Ed.M., Ed.D., 1993), where he was also an adjunct instructor. He is principal of Ravena-Coeymans-Selkirk Mid-dle School (New York). His current research is on organizational climate, trust, and authentic principal and teacher behavior.

This book is dedicated to our friend and colleague,
Dennis J. Sabo.
His legacy lives on.

CHAPTER

1

CLIMATE, CULTURE, AND QUALITY

The day-by-day behavior of the immediate superior and of other significant people in the managerial organization communicates something about their assumptions concerning management, which is of fundamental significance. . . . Many subtle behavioral manifestations of managerial attitude create what is often referred to as the "psychological climate."

Douglas McGregor, 1960,
The Human Side of Enterprise

The school workplace has long been of interest to scholars of educational organizations, but the concept has taken on new importance as educational researchers, reformers, and school practitioners have also become fascinated with the topic. The feel or atmosphere of organizations has been examined under a variety of labels including organizational character, milieu, organizational ideology, ecology, field, situation, informal organization, and more recently, climate and culture. Teachers, administrators, and parents readily use such terms as school climate and school culture with

1

ease, yet there is little shared conception of a specific meaning for any of these terms.

Why the allure of these general, abstract, and ambiguous terms? First, they make sense. They capture something real about organizations; schools do have distinctive identities and atmospheres. Moreover, school climate is a component of the effectiveness and reform movement in education. Edmonds' (1979) early model of effective schools, for example, posited that a school climate composed of strong administrative leadership, high performance expectations, a safe and orderly environment, an emphasis on basic skills, and a system of monitoring student progress promoted high academic achievement. Thus, positive school climate has become part of the effective school rhetoric and is advocated by educational practitioners and reformers as a specific means for improving student achievement.

Two persistent problems remain. First, there is no common understanding of the meaning of school climate; in fact, rhetorical use of climate has obscured the meaning of the concept. Second, there is little systematic empirical evidence linking school climate as a scientific construct with academic achievement (Purkey & Smith, 1983; Ralph & Fennessy, 1983; Rowan, Bossert, & Dwyer, 1983). Until school climate is carefully defined and its dimensions mapped and measured, little progress will be made in determining which aspects of climate are directly related to student outcomes.

Positive school climate is not only a potential means to improve schools, it is an important concept in its own right. The extent to which the school atmosphere promotes openness, colleagueship, professionalism, trust, loyalty, commitment, pride, academic excellence, and cooperation is critical in developing a productive work environment for teachers and administrators. In addition, the extent to which schools are pleasant places to work and learn is meaningful itself. Thus, we view the climate of a school as a probable means for making schools more productive as well as an important end in itself.

The Workplace

There is a variety of ways to conceptualize the nature of the workplace. It should be clear from the preceding brief introduction that we view organizational climate as one such useful perspective. The following chapters of this book are devoted to developing two climate perspectives for analyzing and measuring important dimensions of the workplace of middle schools. We emphasize the middle school for two basic reasons. First, middle schools have been neglected as a domain of study despite the fact that they are an important part of contemporary American education (Carnegie Task Force on Young Adolescents, 1989). Second, our earlier research (Hoy, Tarter, & Kottkamp, 1991) had focused on elementary and high schools; now was the time for middle schools.

Organizational climate is not the only way to view the atmosphere of school; in fact, organizational culture also has received widespread public notoriety (Deal & Kennedy, 1982; Ouchi, 1981; Pascale & Athos, 1981; Peters & Waterman, 1982) as well as serious attention among organizational theorists and researchers (Denison, 1996; Kilmann, Saxton, Serpa, & Associates, 1985; Ouchi & Wilkins, 1985; Schein, 1985, 1990, 1992; Schneider, 1990). With the publication of two "best sellers," Ouchi's (1981) *Theory Z* and Peters and Waterman's (1982) *In Search of Excellence,* the concept of organizational culture was propelled into contemporary thought as a model for examining effective organizations. Not surprisingly, organizational culture has become part of the language of both business and education. Because the use of climate and culture has become commonplace in the discussion and study of schools, each concept is defined and then the two are compared.[1]

Organizational Climate

The concept of organizational climate originated in the late 1950s as social scientists studied variations in work environments. Although researchers interested in educational organizations (Halpin, 1966; Halpin & Croft, 1962, 1963; Pace & Stern, 1958) were pioneers in their efforts to define and measure dimensions of organizational climate, the usefulness of the concept was soon recognized by scholars of business organizations (Taguiri, 1968).

Climate was initially used as a general notion to express the enduring quality of organizational life. Taguiri (1968, p. 23) observes that "a particular configuration of enduring characteristics of the ecology, milieu, social system, and culture would constitute a climate, as much as a particular configuration of personal characteristics constitute a personality." Gilmer (1966, p. 57) specifies organizational climate as "those characteristics that distinguish the

organization from other organizations and that influence the behavior of people in the organization." Litwin and Stringer (1968,
p. 1) suggest that perception is a critical ingredient of climate and
define it as "a set of measurable properties of the work environment,
based on the collective perceptions of the people who live and work
in the environment and demonstrated to influence their behavior."
According to Gilmer (1966), the notion of psychological climates was
introduced in the industrial psychology literature by Gellerman
(1959), but other writers (Forehand & Gilmer, 1964; Halpin & Croft,
1963; Koys & Decotiis, 1991; Taguiri, 1968) have also noted that
definitions of climate are quite similar to early descriptions of personality types. In fact, the climate of an organization may roughly be
conceived as the "personality" of the organization; that is, climate is
to organization as personality is to individual.

Hoy and Miskel (1996, p. 141) synthesize these various perspectives and define *school climate* as a relatively enduring quality of
school environment that is experienced by participants, affects their
behaviors, and is based on their collective perceptions of behavior in
schools.

Organizational Culture

Organizational culture has also become a vehicle for understanding the basic meaning and character of institutional life. Concern for the culture of the workplace also has a rich history. In the
1930s and 1940s, both Barnard (1938) and Mayo (1945) stressed the
significance of norms, sentiments, values, and emergent interactions
in the workplace as they described the nature and function of the
informal organization. Similarly, Selznick (1957) emphasized the significance of viewing organizations as institutions rather than merely
rational organizational structures. Institutions, observes Selznick
(1957, p. 17), are "infused with value beyond the technical requirements at hand." The infusion of value produces a distinctive identity
of the organization that pervades all aspects of organizational life
and provides a social integration that goes well beyond formal coordination and command. This distinctive character binds the individual to the organization and generates in its members a sense of
loyalty and commitment to the organization.

Organizational culture is also an attempt to capture the basic feel
or sense of the organization, but it brings with it conceptual complexity and diversity. No intact definition of culture from anthropol-

ogy or sociology readily lends itself for use as an organizational construct. Understandably, there are a variety of definitions of the term. For example, Ouchi (1981, p. 41) sees organizational culture as "systems, ceremonies, and myths that communicate the underlying values and beliefs of the organization to its employees." Lorsch (1985, p. 84), on the other hand, defines culture as "the beliefs top managers in a company share about how they should manage themselves and other employees." To Mintzberg (1983, p. 152) culture is the organization's ideology, that is, "a system of beliefs about the organization, shared by its members, that distinguishes it from other organizations." Meyerson (1991, p. 256) notes that culture is a "code word for the subjective side of organizational life," whereas Martin (1985, p. 95) asserts that "culture is an expression of people's deepest needs, a means of endowing their experiences with meaning." Schwartz and Davis (1981, p. 33) define culture as "a pattern of beliefs and expectations shared by the organization's members" that "produces norms that powerfully shape the behavior of individuals or groups in organizations." In contrast, Schein (1985, 1990) argues that culture should be reserved for the deeper level of shared assumptions and beliefs of organizational members that operate unconsciously and define an organization's basic view of itself and its environment.

Although differences exist in conceptions, there is some common ground for defining culture. Organizational culture is composed of shared perspectives by the members of the workplace. Some scholars concentrate on shared norms (Kilman et al., 1985), others emphasize shared values (Ouchi, 1981; Peters & Waterman, 1982), and still others focus on common tacit assumptions (Schein, 1985, 1990). Many students of organizational culture are beginning to agree that culture is the deep structure of organizations, which is anchored in the values, beliefs, and assumptions held by organizational participants (Denison, 1996). For our purposes, we define *organizational culture* as a system of shared orientations (norms, core values, and tacit assumptions) held by members, which holds the unit together and gives it a distinctive identity (Hoy & Miskel, 1996).

Climate or Culture?

Which is a more useful framework for the study and analysis of the school workplace? It depends. Both are attempts to identify sig-

nificant properties of organizations. Both are general concepts that
have been defined in numerous ways. Both are somewhat ambiguous; moreover, definitions of climate and culture are often
blurred.

A useful distinction is that culture consists of shared assumptions and ideologies, whereas climate is defined by shared perceptions of behavior (Ashforth, 1985). To be sure, the conceptual leap
from shared assumptions (culture) to shared perceptions (climate) is
not large, but the difference is real and seems meaningful. If the purpose of the analysis is to determine the underlying forces that
motivate behavior in organizations or to focus on the language and
symbolism of the organization, then a cultural approach seems
preferable. But if the aim is to describe perceptions of behavior of
organizational members with the purpose of managing and changing it, then a climate approach seems more desirable.

The two approaches, culture and climate, come from different
intellectual traditions. Scholars of climate use quantitative techniques
and multivariate analyses to identify patterns of perceived behavior
in organizations. They often assume that organizations are rational
instruments to accomplish a purpose; thus, they search for rational
patterns. Their background and training are more likely to be in multivariate statistics and psychology or social psychology rather than
in ethnography and anthropology or sociology. Moreover, these researchers tend to be interested in climate as an independent variable,
that is, how climate influences organizational outcomes. The goal of
studying climate is often to determine effective strategies of change
and the impact that organizations have on groups and individuals
(Koys & Decotiis, 1991).

In contrast, scholars of organizational culture tend to use the
qualitative and enthnograhpic techniques of anthropology and
sociology to examine the character or atmosphere of organizations.
Cultural analysis derives from two basic intellectual traditions:
holistic studies in the tradition of Radcliffe-Brown (1952) and
Malinowski (1961), which focus on the organization as a whole and
how its cultural elements function to maintain a social structure; and
semiotic studies in the tradition of Geertz (1973) and Goodenough
(1971), which focus on language and symbolism. Some who study
culture take a natural-systems view of organizations and conclude
that the culture of an organization is a natural outgrowth of a particular time and place. As such, it is not responsive to attempts at mani-

pulation and change (Ouchi & Wilkins, 1985). Moreover, culture researchers are more concerned with the evolutionary nature of the social system rather than the culture at a given moment (Pettigrew, 1979; Schein, 1990).

In brief, studies of climate usually deal with perceptions of behavior, use survey research techniques, employ multivariate statistics, have their intellectual roots in industrial and social psychology, assume a rational-systems perspective, examine climates as they exist, and are interested in using the knowledge to improve organizations. In contrast, studies of culture typically focus on assumptions, values, and norms, use ethnographic techniques, typically eschew quantitative analysis, have their intellectual roots in anthropology and sociology, assume a natural-systems perspective, and are concerned with the meanings of system symbols and their evolution. There are, of course, exceptions to these patterns, but they do seem to be the dominant ones in the general literature on organizations as well as in specific work on educational organizations (Anderson, 1982; Denison, 1996; Miskel & Ogawa, 1988; Ouchi & Wilkins, 1985). Basic differences between organizational climate and culture are presented in Table 1.1.

Organizational climate is the primary framework we choose to analyze the nature of schools in this book. Our concerns are pragmatic. How can one change the behavior of teachers and principals to make schools more effective? What dimensions of climate best explain the achievement of students? What aspects of student, teacher, and principal behavior are related to excellence, openness, and the quality of school life in general? How can one systematically and efficiently examine the work and managerial atmospheres of schools? We use the research techniques and multivariate statistical methods of industrial and social psychologists to discover answers to these queries. To that end, two contrasting yet complementary perspectives of school climate and their respective measures are developed in this book.

Two Perspectives on School Climate: Using Personality and Health Metaphors

A number of instruments have been systematically developed to examine the organizational climate of schools (Halpin & Croft, 1963;

TABLE 1.1 A Comparison of Perspectives of Organizational
             Climate and Organizational Culture

	Climate	Culture
Discipline:	Psychology and social psychology	Anthropology and sociology
Method:	Survey research, multivariate statistics	Ethnographic techniques, linguistic analysis
Time orientation:	Snapshot of present	Evolutionary and historical view
Level of analysis:	Concrete and less subjective	Abstract and more subjective
Content:	Perceptions of behavior	Shared assumptions and ideology

Hoy & Clover, 1986; Hoy, Hoffman, Sabo, & Bliss, 1996; Hoy et al., 1991; Likert, 1961, 1967; Pace & Stern, 1958; Stern, 1970). One perspective has been to view climate as the "personality" of the school and examine the degree of its openness. Another frame is to examine climate in terms of health. The idea of positive and healthy relations in an organization is not new and calls attention to conditions that foster positive organizational outcomes (Miles, 1969).

Both perspectives, openness and health, have been used to develop contemporary measures of organizational climate in elementary and high schools (Hoy et al., 1991). Our focus in this book is the middle school, an organizational structure that is a hybrid, with the trappings of both elementary and high schools, yet different in its philosophy, grade configuration, and structure.

Climate as Personality

Undoubtedly the best-known conceptualization and measurement of organizational climate in schools is the pioneering study of elementary schools by Halpin and Croft (1962, 1963). Their approach was to identify the critical aspects of teacher-teacher and teacher-principal interactions in schools. To that end, they constructed the Organizational Climate Descriptive Questionnaire (OCDQ), which portrays the climate of an elementary school. School climate is construed as organizational "personality." Indeed, in conceptualizing the climates of schools along an open-to-closed continuum, Halpin and Croft were influenced by Milton Rokeach's (1960) analysis of personality types.

Given the fact that the early work on the OCDQ was the impetus for our development and analysis of school climate, we discuss in some detail the development of the original OCDQ to help the reader understand the basis of subsequent decisions in the refinement of the revised versions of the climate measures. The methods employed in constructing the questionnaires, the assumptions undergirding the approach, and some of the weaknesses and limitations are explained. Our discussion of the OCDQ is drawn heavily from Halpin and Croft's (1962) U.S. Office of Education research report.

An Overview of the OCDQ. The OCDQ is an attempt to map and measure the domain of the climates of elementary schools along a continuum from open to closed. The instrument is composed of 64 Likert-type items, which teachers and principals use to describe the interaction patterns in their schools. The items are short, simple descriptive statements that measure eight dimensions of organizational life. Four of the dimensions or subtests refer to characteristics of the group and four pertain to the characteristics of the principal as leader. The eight dimensions are as follows:

Characteristics of the Group
  1. Disengagement
  2. Hindrance
  3. Esprit
  4. Intimacy

Behavior of the Leader
  5. Aloofness
  6. Production emphasis
  7. Thrust
  8. Consideration

The names of the subtests suggest the behavior that each taps.

School profiles of the eight dimensions were examined to determine if basic patterns existed. They did. Six configurations were identified and arrayed along a rough continuum. The open climate was portrayed as one low on disengagement, low on hindrance, high on esprit, average on intimacy, low on aloofness, low on production emphasis, high on thrust, and high on consideration; the closed climate had the opposite profile. Intermediary climates of autonomous, controlled, familiar, and paternal were also identified and described in terms of the eight dimensions and the relative degree of openness in the interaction patterns. The prototypic profiles for these six climates are summarized in Table 1.2.

Research Strategy. The development of the OCDQ was prompted by four reasons:

- Schools differ markedly in their "feel."
- Morale does not adequately capture this difference in tone.
- Talented principals who take jobs in schools where improvement is necessary are often immobilized by a recalcitrant faculty.
- The notion of the "personality" of a school is intriguing in itself. Obviously, a climate profile should be helpful to administrators and teachers as they seek to improve the atmospheres of their schools.

The general approach used to conceptualize and measure the organizational climate of schools was empirical and statistical. Halpin and Croft developed an extensive set of descriptive items to identify important aspects of teacher and administrative behavior. A guiding assumption of the research was that a desirable organizational climate is one in which leadership acts emerge easily, from whatever source. If a school, or any organization for that matter, is to accomplish its tasks, leadership is essential; but leadership acts can be initiated by the formal leader or by the teachers. Thus, items were written that describe the behavior of the teachers interacting with each other as well as teacher-principal interactions. Teachers and administrators were asked to respond to Likert-type items that characterized behavior in their school; they were asked to indicate the extent to which each stated behavior occurred in their school. The following are typical examples of the items:

- The principal is in the building before teachers arrive.
- Teachers ask nonsensical questions at faculty meetings.
- The rules set by the principal are never questioned.
- Most of the teachers here accept the faults of their colleagues.
- Teachers talk about leaving the school.

The scale used for respondents to record school behavior was defined by the following four categories:

1. Rarely occurs
2. Sometimes occurs
3. Often occurs
4. Very frequently occurs

In constructing the items for the OCDQ, a basic two-pronged requirement was used. The researchers wanted items that would yield a reasonable amount of consensus within a given school, but ones that would also provide discrimination among schools. The ultimate test of the item was empirical; that is, items were subjected to numerous tests, refinements, and iterations. Answers to statements of the type used in the OCDQ are measures of individual perceptions, not fact. Teachers in a school may not, in fact likely will not, agree completely with each other on the behavior patterns in the school. Items that survived the empirical tests were ones that had reasonable consensus. Of course, the question can be raised, "Is that really the behavior of the principal or group?" This is an unanswerable question. Halpin and Croft take the position that how the leader or group really behaves is less important than how its members perceive it. Perceptions of behavior motivate action. Hence, the organizational climate of a school is the faculty's consensus in perception of school behavior. It is assumed that the consensus represents a dependable index of "what is out there" and is instrumental in influencing organizational behavior.

Using a series of empirical, conceptual, and statistical tests, the initial 1,000 descriptive statements in the item bank were drastically reduced, until on the fourth iteration of the instrument, 64 items remained and comprised the final version of the OCDQ (Halpin & Croft, 1962). This version of the measure was administered to the entire professional staff of 71 elementary schools drawn from 6 different regions of the country. Factor analysis revealed that the 64 items could be grouped into 8 factors or subtests. Four of the subtests referred to the characteristics of the faculty group (Disengagement, Hindrance, Esprit, and Intimacy) and four described aspects of the principal-teacher interactions (Aloofness, Production Emphasis, Consideration, and Thrust). These clusters of items provide the eight critical dimensions of organizational climate. Taken together, the eight subtest scores map the climate profile of a given school.

After the profiles were determined for each of the schools, Halpin and Croft used factor analytic techniques to identify 6 basic clusters of profiles; that is, the 71 elementary schools were grouped into 6 categories such that the school climate profiles in each set were similar. Thus, six basic school climates were arrayed along a rough continuum from open to closed: open, autonomous, controlled, familiar, paternal, and closed. For each of the six climate types, a prototypic profile was developed. Table 1.2 outlines the patterns of these six prototypic profiles.

Using the characteristics of the prototypes, it is possible to sketch a behavioral picture of each climate type. We illustrate with the two extreme climate types.

The Open and Closed Climates. The distinctive character of an open climate is its high degree of thrust and esprit and low disengagement. This combination suggests a climate in which both the principal and faculty are genuine and open in their interactions. The principal leads by example (thrust), providing the proper blend of direction and support dependent on the situation. Teachers work well together (esprit) and are committed to the task at hand (low disengagement). Given the "reality-centered" and considerate leadership of the principal as well as the commitment of the faculty, there is no need for burdensome paperwork (hindrance), close supervision (production emphasis), or impersonality and a plethora of rules and regulations (aloofness). Leadership develops easily and appropriately as it is needed. An open school climate is preoccupied with neither task achievement nor social needs, but both emerge freely. In brief, behavior of both the principal and faculty are authentic.

The closed climate is the antithesis of the open. Thrust and esprit are low and disengagement is high. The principal and teachers simply appear to go through the motions (disengagement), with the principal stressing routine trivia and unnecessary busywork

TABLE 1.2 Characteristics of Prototypic Profiles for Each Climate Type

Climate Dimension	Climate Type					
	Open	Autonomous	Controlled	Familiar	Paternal	Closed
Disengagement	Low[a]	Low	Low	High	High	High[a]
Hindrance	Low	Low	High	Low	Low	High
Esprit	High[a]	High	High	Average	Low	Low[a]
Intimacy	Average	High	Low	High	Low	Average
Aloofness	Low	High	High	Low	Low	High
Production emphasis	Low	Low	High	Low	High	High
Thrust	High[a]	Average	Average	Average	Average	Low[a]
Consideration	High	Average	Low	High	High	Low

a. Salient characteristics of open and closed climates.

(hindrance), rules and regulations (aloofness), and unconcern (low consideration). The teachers respond with minimal levels—low morale (esprit) and a lack of commitment (disengagement). The principal's ineffective leadership is further seen in authoritarian and controlling behavior (production emphasis), formal declarations and impersonality (aloofness), as well as a lack of consideration and unwillingness to provide a dynamic personal example. These misguided tactics, which are not taken seriously by the faculty, produce teacher frustration and apathy. They lead to an atmosphere of "game playing" in which the behavior of both the principal and teachers in the closed climate is not genuine; in fact, inauthenticity in teacher and principal behaviors pervades the school.

Criticisms, Weaknesses, and Limitations of the OCDQ. Since the inception of the OCDQ, there has been controversy over the usefulness of the six discrete climates identified by Halpin and Croft. For example, Robert J. Brown's (1965) attempted replication of the OCDQ findings with a sample of Minnesota elementary schools produced eight rather than six climate types; in fact, he argued that although the climate continuum from open to closed might be useful, it was not advisable to place schools into discrete climates. A number of other researchers (Andrews, 1965; Silver, 1983; Watkins, 1968) have also questioned the utility of the discrete climate types. Indeed, Halpin and Croft themselves were circumspect about the clarity of the "middle climates" and described the placing of the six climate types along the open-to-closed continuum as a crude ranking.

An alternative to categorizing schools into discrete climates is to determine the relative openness or closedness of the climate. That is, an index of openness of school climate can be created by adding the esprit and thrust scores for each school and then subtracting from that sum the disengagement score; the higher the score, the more open the climate of the school (Hoy & Miskel, 1987). Appleberry and Hoy (1969) demonstrated the validity of this method, and others have used the method to examine the relationship between openness and other variables (Hoy, 1972; Mullins, 1976; Schwandt, 1978).

The OCDQ has also been criticized for not being well suited for the study of urban schools or secondary schools (Carver & Sergiovanni, 1969; Miskel & Ogawa, 1988). Not only is there a problem with the vagueness of the middle climate categories, but the OCDQ was designed to measure the climate of elementary schools, not secondary ones. Secondary schools are different than elementary schools in a number of important ways, for example, size, specialization, and culture. Urban schools are confronted with a host of complicated social, racial, and economic problems not typically encountered in suburbia. Not surprisingly, urban schools and secondary schools invariably have closed climates when the OCDQ is used.

Paula Silver (1983) argued that the conceptual framework of the OCDQ lacks a clear logic, is cumbersome, and lacks parsimony. For example, although the hindrance subtest is described as a dimension of teacher behavior, it refers to administrative demands rather than interpersonal behavior of teachers. Other conceptual problems plague the instrument. Production emphasis is mislabeled; it measures close, autocratic control by the principal, not an emphasis on high production standards. Directive or controlling behavior is a more apt description of this aspect of principal behavior. Halpin and Croft (1962) themselves question the adequacy of the concept of consideration by suggesting that two or more facets of considerate behavior have been confounded within a single measure.

It is also strange to describe the climate of an organization and not deal with the prime participants—in this case, the students. Perhaps the OCDQ is a measure of administrative or managerial climate. Clearly the focus is on teacher-teacher and teacher-administrator behaviors and not on teacher-student or student-student interactions.

The OCDQ has spawned hundreds of studies during the past three decades. Times and conditions have changed dramatically since the appearance of the OCDQ, yet there has been little effort to revise the instrument. Many of the items, however, no longer measure what they were intended to measure; some of the subtests are no longer valid (e.g., aloofness); the reliabilities of some of the subtests are low; and time has rendered many of the items irrelevant to contemporary school organizations (Hayes, 1973; Hoy & Miskel, 1987). We describe in detail a contemporary and simplified version of the OCDQ—the OCDQ-RM—specifically developed for the middle school, in the next chapter.

Climate as Health

Another perspective for analyzing the nature of the workplace is organizational health. The health metaphor was initially used by

Matthew Miles (1969) to examine the properties of schools. A healthy organization is one that not only survives in its environment, but continues to grow and prosper over the long term. Implicit in this definition is the idea that healthy organizations manage successfully with disruptive outside forces while effectively directing their energies toward the mission and objectives of the organization. Operations on a given day may be effective or ineffective, but the long-term prognosis is favorable in a healthy organization.

Miles (1969) develops a configuration of healthy organization that consists of ten important properties. The first three aspects reflect the task needs of a social system, the second set of properties describe its maintenance needs, and the final group of characteristics are growth and development needs.

The task needs are goal focus, communication adequacy, and optimal power equalization. Each is briefly summarized.

Goal focus is characteristic of healthy organizations. Participants understand the goals of the organization and accept them as realistic ends. Moreover, the goals are also appropriate, that is, consistent with the demands of the environment; in fact, appropriateness may be the most critical feature. The salient question is always: Is this an appropriate goal given the range of other options?

Communication adequacy is also critical to healthy organizations. Because organizations are typically much more complex than small groups, the communication of information is essential to the well-being of the system. Information needs to travel reasonably well. The system must be relatively distortion free with members easily receiving the information they need to function efficiently. Such an efficient communication system enables the organization to sense internal strain and conflict and then promptly deal with them.

Optimal power equalization is the equitable distribution of power and influence. Subordinates exert influence upward and they perceive that their superiors can do likewise. The exertion of influence, however, rests on competence and knowledge rather than position, charisma, or other factors not related to the problem at hand. Collaboration rather than coercion imbues the healthy organization.

A second group of properties deals with the internal state of the organization, specifically with the maintenance needs of its members. These elements are resource use, cohesiveness, and morale.

Resource use deals with effective and efficient use of resources, especially personnel. There is minimal internal strain; the people are neither overloaded nor idle. The fit between the personal needs of participants and the role demands of the organization is good. People in healthy organizations like their jobs and have a positive sense that they are learning and growing as they contribute to the organization.

Cohesiveness refers to a clear sense of identity participants have with the organization. Healthy organizations have members who are attracted to the organization, take pride in their membership, and wish to remain. They are influenced by the organization and exert their influence in a collaborative fashion. In brief, they are proud of the organization and glad they are part of it.

Morale is a group concept. It is the sum of individual sentiments, centered around feelings of well-being and satisfaction as contrasted with feelings of discomfort and dissatisfaction. In healthy organizations, the dominant personal response of organizational members is a sense of well-being.

Finally, there are four more properties of organizational health. Innovativeness, autonomy, adaptation, and problem-solving adequacy deal with the organization's needs for growth and change.

Innovativeness is the organization's ability to invent new procedures, move to new goals and objectives, and become more differentiated over time. Healthy organizations invent new procedures when confronted with problems, procedures that enable them to move toward new objectives, produce new products, and diversify themselves. Such systems grow, develop, and change rather than remain formalized and standardized.

Autonomy describes the organization's relationship with its environment. Healthy organizations do not respond either passively or destructively to the environment. Rather, they demonstrate an ability to remain somewhat independent from negative forces in the environment; they use the environment constructively.

Adaptation is closely related to autonomy. Healthy organizations have effective contact with their surroundings. When environmental forces do not match organizational objectives, a problem-solving and restructuring strategy emerges to cope with the issue. In short, the organization has the ability to bring about corrective changes in itself.

Problem-solving adequacy describes the way organizations handle their difficulties. All organizations, indeed all social systems, have problems and strains. Healthy organizations, just as healthy people, have troubles. Argyris (1964) suggests that effective systems solve their problems with minimal difficulty, and once solved, they stay solved. In the process, problem-solving mechanisms are not weakened but rather strengthened.

Organizational Health of Schools. One of the earliest published attempts to measure school health using Miles' (1969) conceptual framework was performed by Kimpston and Sonnabend (1975). Using the 10 critical dimensions of organizational health, they developed an Organizational Health Description Questionnaire (OHDQ). Likert-type items were written to measure each of the dimensions of health—five items for each dimension. A factor analysis of the instrument, however, was disappointing. Only five interpretable factors were identified and, of Miles' dimensions, only the autonomy and innovativeness were found in pure form. The other three factors were combinations of Miles' properties; for example, a factor called decision making contained optimal power equalization and problem-solving ability items, and school-community relations was a combination of communication adequacy and resource use. In fact, of the 50 items comprising the OHDQ, 30 did not load clearly on any of the 5 factors determined by the factor analysis and were discarded.

Clearly, there are some serious problems with this instrument. Only five of the dimensions were found as expected. The subtests measuring the two pure dimensions of health, autonomy and innovativeness, were unreliable. A reliability coefficient of .48 was reported for autonomy, and for innovativeness the error variance was greater than the individual variance. Indeed, except for the factor called interpersonal relations, a three-item variable composed of morale and cohesiveness items (reliability coefficient = .72), all of the subtests of the instrument had exceedingly low reliabilities. Moreover, no validity evidence is provided for any of the subtests. Miles (1975), himself, while applauding their effort, notes many of the same reservations about Kimpston and Sonnabend's (1975) organizational health questionnaire.

There have been other attempts to operationalize Miles' perspective on organizational health. Fairman and his colleagues (Childers

& Fairman, 1985; Clark & Fairman, 1983) at the University of Arkansas have developed an Organizational Health Instrument that they use in inservice activities with schools. Unfortunately, their instrument seems to suffer from many of the same psychometric problems that have been described.

The literature points to a number of difficulties in the development of the school health inventory. First, the 10 characteristics proposed by Miles may not be mutually exclusive. Second, it is no easy feat to construct a measure of organizational health that is reliable and valid. Third, the appropriate unit of analysis for developing an organizational health instrument for schools is the organization, not the individual. Unfortunately, most early developers of health instruments used the individual. Finally, factor analysis is no substitute for sound theory and careful and extensive pilot work.

A strong conceptual base as well as series of empirical tests and factor analyses are essential to build a reliable and valid measure of organizational health. Given the lack of success of early attempts to operationalize school health, we shifted the theoretical underpinnings of the health construct from the work of Miles to that of Parsons (1951, 1961, 1967). We describe in detail the theoretical foundations, the development, and the test of a reliable and valid measure of school health for the middle level in Chapter 3.

Quality Schools

Quality has joined organizational effectiveness as a concept used to assess organizations; in fact, some scholars argue that it has replaced effectiveness (Cameron & Whetten, 1995). Effectiveness invariably refers only to the products or outputs of the organization, while in contrast, the notion of quality is not tied to products. Rather, it deals with the quality of the entire system—all of its components—the internal processes as well as the products.

The emphasis on quality in the contemporary organizational literature can be traced to the popularity of the work of W. Edwards Deming (1983, 1986, 1993) on total quality management (TQM). After World War II, Deming and his philosophy of management turned around Japanese industry and helped make Japan a dominant business force in the postwar world. Japan set a new standard for industry and business success, and by the 1980s, more and more American business, governmental, and service organizations were turning to Deming's teachings, philosophy, and his principles of total quality management.

Like effectiveness, the concept of quality is difficult to define, but a number of concepts that undergird quality organizations emerge from the writing of Deming and his followers. We prefer the construct of quality over effectiveness because it is a broader term that includes the elements of the organization and not simply outcomes. One way to come to a fuller understanding of quality in organizations is to examine the basic principles that Deming (1986) advances to transform organizations into quality institutions. We turn briefly to those principles.

Principles of Total Quality Management (TQM)

The quality approach can be summarized as a set of 14 principles for transforming and improving organization and administration. These principles of transformation represent a complex, prescriptive set of interrelated rules stated in terms of a series of commands. Increasingly, educational administrators and educational commentators (American Association of School Administrators, 1991; Bonstingl, 1994; Glaub, 1990; Leonard, 1991; Meany, 1991; Rhodes, 1990) believe that the notion of quality and total quality management are useful for schools, but some remain skeptical (Capper & Jamison, 1993; Pallas & Neuman, 1993). Each of the TQM principles is summarized and applied to schools.

1. *Create a constant purpose of improvement.* Schools must never be content to rest on their laurels; they must constantly be studying themselves and changing in ways that improve teaching and learning. Improvement is a continuous process.

2. *Adopt a philosophy of change and improvement.* Administrators need to engage in leadership of change, which means continuous research, planning, evaluation, and improvement.

3. *Avoid close supervision and ratings to achieve quality.* Close supervision and teacher ratings do not produce long-term improvement in teaching and learning; in fact, such supervision is likely to create an atmosphere of suspicion and hostility rather than teacher commitment and openness.

4. *Avoid decisions that produce short-term benefits at the expense of long-term consequences.* New ideas and novel approaches should not be eliminated on the basis of cost alone. Cost should not be the bottom line in educational decisions—quality should be. Smaller classes, newer technology, and teacher aids are simply a few examples of issues that may have long-term positive effects on student learning. Short-term costs may be high, but long-term benefits may be great.

5. *Improve all aspects of the school social system, not simply the classroom.* The quality of the education produced by the school is a function of the harmony within and among its subsystems. Cooperation and teamwork are necessary both within and among the systems, that is, between the school and parents, between the board and the administration, between administrators and teachers, and between teachers and students.

6. *Initiate opportunities for professional development.* Continued education is necessary for everyone, but new employees especially need on-the-job education. Beginning teachers are often uneasy and sometimes unprepared for the rigors of teaching. Inservice programs will not only save much grief but should help beginners develop the security they need to perform well in the classroom. Inservice training is wasted, however, if administrative action is uninformed and insensitive.

7. *Institute transformational leadership.* A school principal must be a leader with vision, one that stresses the development of human capital. A prime responsibility of principals is to develop in their professional staffs an ethic of continual self-improvement, a pride in teaching, and a focus on quality. In the final analysis, the only people who can change the instruction in the classroom are the teachers themselves. Ultimately the teacher must decide what changes are needed to improve student learning. Such change cannot be mandated; it must grow from within the professional. Principals cannot simply be managers. They must be leaders who can build a culture of openness, trust, collegiality, confidence, and introspection among their teachers (Hoy & Forsyth, 1986).

8. *Drive out fear.* Mediocrity is the result when fear permeates the organization (Scherkenbach, 1992). People need to be

secure if they are to perform well; they need to ask important questions, to challenge accepted practices, to take risks, and to be innovative. Put simply, if we want teachers to grow, experiment, and continue to improve their professional practices, then we must drive out fear and create a school climate of trust and mutual respect.

9. *Break down barriers between departments.* Teamwork and openness are hallmarks of quality. Teachers and administrators together need to attack the complex problem of improving teaching and learning. Teachers can ill afford to isolate themselves in the confines of traditional departments. Schools must avoid artificial barriers that inhibit cooperation and teamwork. Organizational features that foster isolation and extreme specialization are counterproductive to quality in schools.

10. *Eliminate slogans and exhortations that mask problems.* Many exhortations mask administrative responsibility and organizational impediments and highlight teacher shortcomings. Such slogans also generate frustration, cynicism, and resentment among teachers who see administrators as either being naive about the complexity of their problems or, worse, as hiding behind a cloak of authority. When problems exist, slogans can always be found to mask the causes; slogans are not solutions.

11. *Eliminate management by numerical standards.* Such standards are typically obstacles to quality and productivity because they tend to cap improvement. Once a teacher has reached the standard, there is little motivation to continue to advance. When effectiveness is judged by achieving some magical number, understanding of the job is subordinated to attaining a quota. This is not a system that fosters continual improvement; it is a mechanical process that has negative consequences for quality. To use Deming's (1986) words, "Management by numerical goal is an attempt to manage without knowledge of what to do, and in fact is usually management by fear" (p. 76).

12. *Remove barriers that rob teachers of the pride of teaching.* If school administrators want to meet student needs and fulfill

parental expectations, they must examine their administrative practices and procedures with an eye to eliminating those that inhibit continuing improvement. Avoid practices and procedures that focus attention on end products rather than people and processes, which are keys to system success.

13. *Institute a program of education and self-improvement.* The school should be a laboratory for learning at all levels—student, teacher, and administrator. If there is one principle schools should excel in, it is to provide all members with a sound program of training, education, and self-improvement. To be true to the Deming philosophy, such on-the-job education should be anchored in fostering teamwork and cooperation. It may be no accident that cooperative learning is one of the most widely respected and successful contemporary teaching innovations in schools today (Slavin, 1991).

14. *Put everyone to work transforming the organization.* Implementing the previous 13 principles is no simple feat. School administrators and teachers must first understand and agree with the new responsibilities of a quality approach; then everybody must transform the organization. The essence of the approach is improvement; in fact, half of the TQM directives are focused on improving processes (Principles 1, 2, 5, 6, 7, 13, 14), and the other half are directed at removing obstacles to improvement (Principles 3, 4, 8, 9, 10, 11, 12).

In brief, quality schools have as their purpose the continual improvement of learning and teaching. A school climate that emphasizes cooperation, trust, openness, and continuous improvement is essential for quality schools. Education and professional development for teachers and administrators are keys to improvement and self-regulated learning.

Some Indicators of Quality Schools

This brief review of principles of quality management provides a rough framework of organizational properties that are indicators of school quality. Thus we turn to a set of concepts that undergirds a quality approach for schools.

First, the concepts of climate openness and health as they will be framed in this book are indicators of quality schools. Openness of the leadership of the principal is marked by support for teachers, freedom and encouragement for teachers to experiment and act independently, and few, if any, restrictive bureaucratic procedures. Openness of teacher behavior refers to teachers who are serious and engaged in teaching, are committed to their students, and are professional, accepting, and mutually respectful of each other.

Organizational health is another index of school quality. Health refers to the positive linkages and harmony within and between key elements in the school. In particular, healthy interpersonal dynamics between administrators and teachers and between teachers and students are key elements of quality schools. They include such aspects as dynamic leadership, academic emphasis, adequate resources, teacher affiliation, as well as a professional orientation that is geared toward self-regulation and continuous improvement.

If the health and openness of school climate are indicators of quality, then they should be related to excellence in other organizational activities and outcomes that meet general expectations of parents, teachers, and the public at large. In schools, student achievement is clearly one outcome that virtually everyone agrees is desirable. Schools have as one of their goals teaching students how to read, write, and do mathematics; hence, student achievement is another measure of school quality.

Likewise, quality and effectiveness should be highly related. Although effectiveness is not an easy term to define, most people would agree that in addition to student achievement, schools should be efficient, flexible, and adaptable. Moreover, perceived global indicators of effectiveness of schools are available and should be related to measures of school quality.

Finally, the culture of schools should be related to quality. In particular, shared identity, trust, authenticity, cooperation, and participation should be key values that pervade quality schools. This list of quality indicators is not exhaustive; in fact, we are certain that other quality indicators should be considered. We focus on this set of concepts (see Table 1.3) because these are ones for which we have systematic data—ones that we will examine in more detail in the chapters to follow.

TABLE 1.3 Some Indicators of School Quality

Openness of school climate
- Openness of leadership
- Openness of teacher behavior

Health of school climate
- Dynamic leadership
- Academic emphasis
- Resource support
- Teacher affiliation
- Professional orientation

Student achievement
- Reading
- Mathematics
- Writing

Overall school effectiveness
- Quality and quantity of products and services
- Efficiency
- Flexibility
- Adaptability

Culture
- Shared identity
- Trust
- Authenticity
- Cooperation
- Participation

Summary

In this introductory chapter, we have laid the foundations for the rest of the book. First, the concepts of organizational culture and organizational climate were defined, compared, and contrasted. Then, two perspectives of school climate were formulated: openness and health. A brief historical look at each framework provided the background and conceptual underpinnings for the development of measures for each view. Next, the concepts of total quality management and school quality were discussed and elaborated. Finally, we concluded the chapter with a set of empirical indicators of school quality. In the next chapter, we detail the conceptual foundations for the Organizational Climate Description Questionnaire for Middle Schools, explicate the research strategy to develop the instrument, provide the technical details of the investigation, and test and specify the reliability and validity of the instrument.

Note

1. We have drawn heavily on three sources (Hoy, 1990; Hoy & Miskel, 1996; Hoy et al., 1991) for our analysis of climate, culture, and school quality.

CHAPTER

2

THE ORGANIZATIONAL CLIMATE DESCRIPTION QUESTIONNAIRE FOR MIDDLE SCHOOLS

Anyone who visits more than a few schools notes quickly how schools differ from each other in their "feel." In one school the teachers and the principal are zestful and exude confidence. . . . In a second school the brooding discontent of the teachers is palpable; the principal tries to hide his incompetence and his lack of a sense of direction behind a cloak of authority, and yet he wears this cloak poorly because the attitude he displays to others vacillates randomly between the obsequious and the officious.

Andrew W. Halpin, 1966,
Theory and Research in Administration

Just as individuals have personalities, so too do schools. It is this "personality" of the school that Halpin (1966) described as the organizational climate of the school. In the last chapter, we briefly described Halpin's development of the Organizational Climate Description Questionnaire (OCDQ) for elementary schools, an instrument that is over 30 years old. In this chapter, we detail the development of a new, contemporary measure of school climate called the Organizational Climate Description Questionnaire (Revised) for Middle Schools (OCDQ-RM),[1] which builds on the work of Halpin (1966) and Hoy, Tarter, and Kottkamp (1991). The organizational climate of elementary and secondary schools has been conceptualized and operationalized in numerous studies (Halpin, 1966; Hoy & Clover, 1986; Hoy et al., 1991; Kottkamp, Mulhern, & Hoy, 1987). The results of that research have demonstrated that elementary and secondary schools are different in many important respects; in fact, different measures are used to tap the dimensions of climate at each level, for example, the Organizational Climate Descriptive Questionnaire for Elementary Schools (OCDQ-RE) and the OCDQ-RS for secondary schools. Most researchers (Ash, 1992; Finneran, 1990) use either the elementary or secondary version to study the organizational climates of middle schools in spite of the fact that both the philosophy and structure of middle schools are relatively distinct.

Middle schools are ubiquitous; they have all but replaced the traditional junior high school. Grade levels in middle schools vary but most often include 5-8, 6-8, or 7-8 grade configurations. The charge, however, that middle schools are nothing more than junior high schools with a different grade configuration is not supported by the research (Cawelti, 1988; Toepfer, 1990). Middle schools have different programs. Typical middle school programs have interdisciplinary team structures, a child-centered philosophy, heterogeneous groupings for most subjects, specialization of subjects, interdisciplinary activities, an appropriate core curriculum, as well as time and flexibility for student exploration and activities structured around the team or unit concept, and teaching strategies geared specifically for young adolescents (Alexander & George, 1981; Cawelti, 1988).

In brief, middle schools are neither elementary schools nor junior nor senior high schools. Neither an instrument designed for the elementary school (e.g., OCDQ-RE) nor one developed for high schools (e.g., OCDQ-RS) seems likely to be adequate for use in middle schools. Hence, the purpose of this chapter is twofold: first, to conceptualize and develop a measure of the organizational climate for middle schools, and then to assess the validity of the OCDQ construct by testing several theoretically derived hypotheses.

Developing a New Climate Measure: The OCDQ-RM

The development of an OCDQ for middle schools had a number of phases:

- Conceptualizing school climate
- Generating items to operationalize the climate construct
- Conducting a pilot study to reduce and refine items and dimensions of school climate
- Conducting a second study to test the stability of the factor structure of the construct
- Testing the reliability of the new middle school instrument (OCDQ-RM)

Conceptual Framework

The organizational climate of a school is the set of internal characteristics that distinguishes one school from another and influences the behavior of its members. In more specific terms, school climate is the relatively stable property of the school environment that is experienced by participants, affects their behavior, and is based on their collective perceptions of behavior in schools (Hoy & Miskel, 1991; Taguiri, 1968).

The theoretical framework for organizational climate for middle schools was based on the work of Halpin (1966) and Hoy and his colleagues (Hoy & Clover, 1986; Hoy & Feldman, 1987; Hoy et al., 1991). Organizational climate was conceived as the "personality" of the school, that is, climate : organization :: personality : individual, and the openness of the climate was conceived as a pivotal second-order characteristic of schools. It was postulated that middle schools could be arrayed along a rough continuum of climates from open to closed.

Open climates have teacher-teacher and teacher-principal interactions that are genuine and open. Teachers as well as principals are "up-front" with each other, supportive, receptive to the ideas of each other, and committed to the task at hand. In contrast, closed school climates are marked by interactions that are guarded, suspicious, controlling, restrictive, distant, and disengaged. "Game playing" and "posturing" imbue the closed climate.

Measuring School Openness

Once it was decided to conceive of middle school climate in terms of openness of principal and teacher behavior, a strategy to generate items to measure climate became clear. Rather than reinvent the construct, we built on earlier work (Halpin, 1966; Hoy & Clover, 1986; Hoy et al., 1991). We started by using all of the items that were on the OCDQ-RE and OCDQ-RS. In effect, the decision was to use an empirical test to see which items from each instrument worked for middle schools. Next, we wrote an additional 16 items designed to capture distinct properties of middle schools. Items were developed by the researchers independently and jointly, but no items were included on the initial instrument unless there was agreement on the following criteria:

- Each item represented an aspect of a middle school.
- Each statement was clear and concise.
- Each statement had content validity.
- Each statement measured one of the climate dimensions.

In all, 72 Likert-type items were used in the preliminary version of the OCDQ-RM. Examples of items added included the following: "The interactions between team-unit members are cooperative"; "Members of teams-units consider other members to be friends"; and " Interdisciplinary units are looked on as burdensome by faculty members." Teachers were asked to indicate the extent to which each statement characterized their school along a 4-point scale from *rarely occurs, sometimes occurs, often occurs,* to *very frequently occurs.*

Pilot Study

To test the factor structure of the new middle school instrument, the OCDQ-PM, a small pilot study was conducted. Seventy-eight teachers from 78 different middle schools responded to the 72-item preliminary questionnaire. The sample of schools represented a diverse set of middle schools in New Jersey in terms of size, socioeconomic status, and ethnicity. The items on the instrument represented eight aspects of school climate—three described principal-teacher interactions (Directive, Restrictive, and Supportive principal behaviors) and five mapped teacher-teacher interactions (Collegial, Intimate, Disengaged, Frustrated, and Engaged teacher behaviors).

A set of exploratory factor analyses (principal components with varimax rotation) of the pilot data was performed. We anticipated a seven-factor solution (disengaged and engaged behavior were conceived as opposite poles of the same dimension). A six-factor solution emerged, however, as the best solution when evaluated against the following criteria:

- Simple structure—items load high on one factor and near zero on the others.
- Conceptual fit—items are theoretically consistent with each other.
- Substantial factor loadings—items had factor loadings of greater than .45.

Using these criteria to refine the measure, 24 of the 72 items were eliminated. That is, those items that did not load strongly on one and only one factor, had weak factor loadings, or did not fit conceptually were deleted.

The final factor analysis in the pilot study was performed on these remaining 48 items. The result yielded six factors that were named Supportive, Directive, and Restrictive principal behavior and Collegial, Committed, and Disengaged teacher behavior. These six factors accounted for 59.2% of all the variance. Unlike elementary and secondary schools, intimacy did not emerge as a unique dimension of middle school climate. Moreover, the concept of committed teacher behavior developed as a distinct property of middle schools. Committed behavior here refers not to commitment of teachers to the school or to their colleagues but commitment of teachers to their students. Reliabilities of four of the six scales were high, but the commitment and disengaged scales had low reliabilities (see Table 2.1).

In sum, six factors were identified. Four of the factor subtests had high reliabilities. Because the commitment and disengagement factors each had low reliabilities and contained only 3 items each, 12 additional items were written for these subtests. Hence, a revised 60-item climate instrument for middle schools was ready for further analysis and refining.

TABLE 2.1 Reliabilities and the Six Scales

	Number of Items	Reliability (alpha)
Supportive principal behavior	11	.93
Collegial teacher behavior	14	.92
Directive principal behavior	9	.85
Restrictive principal behavior	8	.81
Committed teacher behavior	3	.60
Disengaged teacher behavior	3	.46
Total items	48	

The Revised Middle School
Instrument (OCDQ-RM): Another Test

Having completed the preliminary analysis of the instrument, the revised 60-item OCDQ-RM was ready to be tested with a new and more comprehensive set of data. Middle schools in the sample were selected with the aim of

- Demonstrating the stability of the factor structure
- Confirming the validity and stability of the subtests
- Checking for a second-order factor of openness

Sample

A new sample of 87 middle schools, which included responses from 2,777 teachers, was used to refine and confirm the structure of the instrument and then to test several hypotheses about climate and authenticity. The unit of analysis was the school because climate variables reflect organizational properties (Hoy et al., 1991; Sirotnik, 1980).

Although it was not possible to select a random sample of New Jersey middle schools, care was taken to select urban, suburban, and rural schools from diverse geographic areas of the state as well as from all socioeconomic levels in the state. Only schools that called themselves middle schools and had a 5-8, 6-8, or 7-8 configuration were included in the sample. Extremely small middle schools were not part of the sample; schools with fewer than 15 faculty members were not considered for the sample. Using the state's measure of socioeconomic status, 28% of the schools came from the lowest levels, 38% came from the middle levels, and 34% came from the highest levels. Fifteen of the 21 counties in New Jersey were represented in the sample.

Data Collection

Data were collected from teachers at regularly scheduled faculty meetings. The researcher explained the purpose of the study in general terms, guaranteed the anonymity of respondents, and stressed the importance of candid responses. Teachers at the meeting were divided into three random groups with one group responding to the OCDQ-RM, another group describing school health (OHI-M), and still another group completing a separate set of scales, which included measures of teacher and principal authenticity. This procedure was used because the unit of analysis was the school (data were aggregated at the school level) and because it ensured methodological separation of the independent and dependent variables. Virtually everyone in attendance responded to the instruments, but no attempts were made to pursue responses from those absent from the meetings.

Factor Analysis

School mean scores were calculated for each item of the climate instrument, and the item-correlation matrix for the 87 schools was factor analyzed. A principal components factor analysis with a varimax rotation confirmed the 6 predicted climate dimensions; however, 10 of the items failed the test of simple structure—strong loadings on one and only one factor—and were eliminated. Thus the final version of the OCDQ-RM contained 50 items that defined 6 factors of school climate; their eigenvalues ranged from 1.92 to 16.25 explaining 70% of the variance (see Table 2.2).

The results supported the same factor structure found in the pilot study. Three factors captured principal-teacher interactions—Supportive, Directive, and Restrictive behaviors; and Collegial, Committed, and Disengaged behaviors described teacher-teacher interactions. Moreover, the reliability coefficients for all six subtests

TABLE 2.2 Six-Factor Varimax Solution for the 50 Items of the OCDQ-RM (*N* = 87)

Subtest	Item	F1	F2	F3	F4	F5	F6
	01	*.83*	.14	.11	−.34	.03	−.16
	13	*.66*	.14	.05	.02	−.35	−.32
	14	*.89*	.08	.17	−.07	−.12	−.03
Supportive	15	*.77*	.10	.20	−.07	−.10	.01
	18	*.85*	.09	.14	−.10	−.03	−.19
	23	*.85*	.16	.17	−.06	−.04	−.17
	31	*.85*	.13	.17	−.03	−.20	−.09
	39	*.80*	.02	.12	−.07	−.36	−.20
	43	*.88*	.09	.14	−.07	.01	−.14
	52	*.78*	.19	.15	−.10	−.07	−.30
	59	*.69*	.16	.22	−.24	.15	−.01
	08	−.11	*.67*	.38	−.19	−.07	.02
	09	.07	*.59*	.39	−.24	−.05	−.14
	10	.03	*.76*	.30	−.11	−.22	.01
	21	.10	*.83*	.10	−.07	.01	−.11
Committed	22	.20	*.82*	−.02	−.04	.09	.04
	27	.16	*.71*	.02	−.29	−.27	−.03
	55	.06	*.70*	.28	−.19	−.03	−.28
	56	.17	*.72*	.18	−.12	.10	.05
	58	.14	*.85*	.10	−.08	−.07	−.15
	02	.27	.20	*.63*	.10	−.11	.03
	16	.08	.10	*.74*	.15	.10	−.05
	17	.11	.06	*.77*	.20	.08	.10
	19	.19	.41	*.68*	−.11	−.08	−.12
Collegial	29	.10	.05	*.55*	−.17	−.14	−.11
	32	.24	.06	*.69*	.09	−.07	−.06
	41	.34	.30	*.67*	−.12	−.01	−.08
	42	.23	.39	*.52*	−.31	−.16	−.15
	48	.19	.35	*.70*	−.29	−.02	−.13

were high: Supportive (.96), Directive (.88), Restrictive (.89), Collegial (.90), Committed (.93), and Disengaged (.87).

A comparison of the findings of this factor analysis with the pilot results (Table 2.1) shows that the six dimensions are identical and the reliability of the subtests on the final form are higher. Note that the

TABLE 2.2 Continued

Subtest	Item	F1	F2	F3	F4	F5	F6
Collegial	51	.04	.05	.48	−.16	−.19	−.50
	54	.09	.11	.54	−.24	−.07	−.39
	11	−.11	−.09	.12	.61	−.16	.26
	30	.05	.06	−.10	.49	.36	.06
	33	−.06	−.02	−.09	.59	−.18	.35
	34	−.13	−.28	−.39	.67	.05	.04
Disengaged	35	.01	−.03	.25	.71	−.05	.16
	36	−.05	−.19	−.02	.84	.14	−.13
	37	−.13	−.30	−.10	.74	−.10	.06
	38	−.16	−.20	.03	.74	.01	−.02
	60	−.18	−.34	−.31	.60	.13	.22
	12	−.33	−.09	−.11	.05	.63	.10
	24	.21	.02	.01	.04	.81	.05
Directive	40	−.18	−.02	.01	−.12	.66	.20
	44	−.42	−.17	−.13	−.01	.69	.01
	46	−.26	−.02	−.07	.01	.87	.15
	49	−.06	−.11	−.05	−.01	.91	.07
	04	−.34	−.22	−.03	.14	.21	.67
Restrictive	07	−.32	−.04	−.01	.18	−.02	.79
	47	−.36	−.10	−.14	.13	.24	.69
	50	−.24	−.04	−.20	.05	.22	.74
Eigenvalue		16.2	5.63	4.06	3.18	2.77	1.92
Percentage variance		32.5	11.3	8.1	7.6	5.6	3.8

NOTE: Italicized numbers represent the defining factor loadings for each of the subtests.

two weak scales in the pilot study, Committed and Disengaged behavior, now also have high reliabilities, a consequence of the new items added to the instrument. Sample items and the constitutive definition for each dimension of climate are provided in Table 2.3.

TABLE 2.3 Definition and Sample Items for Each Subtest

Supportive principal behavior is directed toward both the social needs and task achievement of faculty. The principal is helpful, genuinely concerned with teachers, and attempts to motivate by using constructive criticism and by setting an example through hard work.

Sample items:
- The principal goes out of his or her way to help teachers.
- The principal uses constructive criticism.
- The principal sets an example by working hard himself or herself.

Directive principal behavior is rigid domineering behavior. The principal maintains close and constant monitoring over virtually all aspects of teacher behavior in the school.

Sample items:
- The principal rules with an iron fist.
- The principal supervises teachers closely.
- The principal monitors everything teachers do.

Restrictive principal behavior is behavior that hinders rather than facilitates teacher work.

Sample items:
- Teachers are burdened with busywork.
- Routine duties interfere with the job of teaching.
- Assigned nonteaching duties are excessive.

Collegial teacher behavior supports open and professional interactions among teachers. Teachers like, respect, and help one another both professionally and personally.

The stability of the factor structure also provides construct-related evidence for the six dimensions of climate. Factor analysis enables the researcher to study the constitutive meanings of constructs. In the current study, six hypothetical dimensions of school climate were postulated and empirically demonstrated. The relations among the items measuring each climate dimension were systematically related to each other as expected in the factor analysis of the OCDQ-RM. The strong loadings in the predicted six-factor solution as well as the high reliabilities of the subtests suggests that the OCDQ-RM is a useful instrument with extremely high reliability. In brief, validity and reliability evidence is strong.[2]

TABLE 2.3 Continued

Sample items:
- Teachers help and support each other.
- Teachers respect the professional competence of their colleagues.
- Teachers provide strong social support for colleagues.

Committed teacher behavior is directed toward helping students to develop both socially and intellectually. Teachers work extra hard to insure student success in school.

Sample items:
- Teachers "go the extra mile" with their students.
- Teachers help students on their own time.
- Teachers are committed to helping their students.

Disengaged teacher behavior signifies a lack of meaning and focus to professional activities. Teachers simply are putting in their time; in fact, they are critical and unaccepting of their colleagues.

Sample items:
- Teachers ramble when they talk at faculty meetings.
- Teachers mock teachers who are different.
- Teachers don't listen to other teachers.

Second-Order Factor Analysis

Thus far, we have been concerned with identifying items that formed the six basic dimensions of middle school climate. Halpin and Croft (1962) propose three standards for evaluating a battery of tests:

- Subtests should measure different types of behavior.
- The battery of tests as a whole should tap enough common behavior to permit researchers to find a pattern of more general factors.
- The general factors extracted should not be discordant with those already reported in the literature.

First, an examination of the correlation matrix among the six subtests (see Table 2.4) demonstrates our success on the first stan-

TABLE 2.4 Intercorrelations of the Six Subtests of the OCDQ-RM

Subtest	1	2	3	4	5	6
1. Supportive principal behavior	(.96)[a]					
2. Directive principal behavior	−.55	(.88)				
3. Restrictive principal behavior	−.44	.42	(.89)			
4. Collegial teacher behavior	.48	−.40	−.28	(.90)		
5. Committed teacher behavior	.36	−.30	−.24	−.25	(.93)	
6. Disengaged teacher behavior	−.27	.36	.10	−.25	−.42	(.87)

a. Alpha coefficients of reliability are reported in the parentheses.

dard; all intercorrelations among the measures were weak to moderate. We now turn to the last two standards to evaluate our efforts.

Based on the extant literature, we had postulated general dimensions of openness undergirding middle school climate. A second-order factor analysis of the six subtests of the OCDQ-RM was therefore performed on the subtest correlation matrix. The theoretical and empirical questions guiding the second-order factor analysis were the following:

- Are there more general factors underlying middle school climate?
- If so, do they represent the notions of openness that have been described in the literature (Halpin, 1966; Hoy & Clover, 1986; Hoy et al., 1991; Kottkamp et al., 1987)?

A factor analysis of the correlation matrix for the six subtests did produce two more general Factors of climate. The two-factor solution with a varimax rotation is given in Table 2.5. Supportive, Directive, and Restrictive principal behavior define Factor I; that is, the subtests load strongly on that factor, whereas Collegial, Committed, and Disengaged teacher behavior load strongly on Factor II.

TABLE 2.5 Two-Factor, Varimax Solution for the Six Dimensions of the OCDQ-RM

Subtest	I *Principal Openness*	II *Teacher Openness*
Supportive	.76	.30
Directive	−.83	.05
Restrictive	−.70	−.32
Collegial	.47	.56
Committed	.23	.78
Disengaged	−.03	−.80

Factor	*Eigenvalue*	*Percentage of Variance*	*Cumulative Variance*
I	2.83	47.2	47.2
II	1.01	16.9	64.1

Factor I is characterized by principal behavior that is friendly, helpful, and constructive (high supportiveness); that encourages teachers to make independent judgments and act as autonomous professionals (low directiveness); and that frees teachers from excessive bureaucratic demands and burdens (low restrictiveness). In general, this factor denotes an openness and functional flexibility in teacher-principal interactions; consequently, it was named "openness in principal behavior." An index of openness in principal behavior can be developed by combining the scores of the three dimensions of principal behavior. The formula for the index is found in Chapter 5.

Factor II is defined by teacher behavior that is friendly, close, supportive, and professional (high collegiality); that is open, helpful, and committed to students (high commitment); and that is meaningful, tolerant, and respectful of other teachers (low disengagement). Factor II also denotes openness and functional flexibility in teacher-teacher and teacher-student interactions; hence, it was called "openness in teacher behavior." Teacher openness can be determined by combining the scores on the three dimensions of Factor II; see Chapter 5 for the formula.

Thus, the OCDQ-RM has two general second-order factors, both viewed along an open-closed continuum—openness of principal behavior and openness of teacher behavior—findings consistent with the extant literature.

Openness and Authenticity:
Some Hypotheses and a Test

The next step in the study was to construct some hypotheses using the notions of climate and openness that had been developed. Halpin (1966) describes a salient feature of openness in the climate of a school as the authenticity of relationships. He argued that in open climates people are real and interactions are genuine; that is, behavior is authentic. In contrast, closed school climates are marked by phony interpersonal relationships; people play games with each other. They merely act out what they believe are appropriate roles; their behavior is inauthentic. Thus it seemed logical to expect that openness in the climate of middle schools should be closely linked to authentic teacher and principal behavior.

Authenticity

Authenticity is a slippery concept. There have been numerous attempts (Brumbaugh, 1971; Halpin, 1966; Henderson & Hoy, 1982; Seeman, 1966) to define the term, with mixed success. For purposes of this study, the framework developed by Henderson and Hoy (1982) is used. Authentic behavior consists of three basic aspects:

- Accountability—the willingness to accept organizational and personal responsibility for mistakes as well as negative outcomes; there is no passing the buck, scapegoating, or blaming others. Responsibility is accepted.
- Nonmanipulation—colleagues or subordinates are not used for one's own purposes.
- Salience of self over role—role is subordinated to self; basic personality is a prime motivator of behavior, not some prescribed role.

In brief, authentic behavior is characterized by a willingness to accept responsibility for behavior, especially when the results are not positive; behavior that is also nonmanipulative of others; and behavior in which role is subordinated to self.

Climate Openness and Authenticity of Behavior

Halpin (1966) was first to note that schools with open climates were distinctive in that what was going on in these schools was "for real," whereas in schools with closed climates, behavior was staged; the teachers seemed to behave according to roles without understanding the meaning of their roles. He vividly states the case:

> In the first situation, the behavior of the principal and teachers seemed genuine, or authentic, and the characters were three dimensional. In the second situation, the behavior of group members seemed to be thin, two dimensional, and stereotyped; we are reminded of papier-mâché characters acting out their roles in a puppet show. Something in the first situation made it possible for the characters to behave authentically—that is, "for real" or genuinely. The professional roles of individuals remained secondary to what the individuals, themselves, were as human beings. (p. 204)

Open climates provide the latitude for individuals to work out their roles and bring their own personalities to bear in the process. Closed climates, on the other hand, are overspecified and provide a cloak that often serves to hide true personal identities. Moreover, in the closed climate, teachers and principals behave ritualistically and in ways that preclude the establishment of authentic relationships (Halpin, 1966). Indeed, Halpin suggests that authenticity is of pivotal importance to the open climate. Thus, openness in behavior of teachers and principals in middle schools should be related to authenticity in their behavior. To examine this proposition as well as to assess the validity of our notion of open and closed climates, we tested the following two hypotheses:

H1   The more open the perceived behavior of principals, the more authentic their behavior will be perceived.

H2   The more open the perceived behavior of teachers, the more authentic their behavior will be perceived.

Moreover, we expected that perceived openness of the principal would not be as strongly related to authenticity in teacher behavior as to authenticity in principal behavior; conversely, perceived openness of teacher behavior would not be as strongly related to authenticity in principal behavior as to authenticity in teacher behavior.

Authenticity Scales

To test these hypotheses, two authenticity scales were administered to a separate random sample of teachers in each school; none of the teachers in the school who had responded to the OCDQ-RM responded to the authenticity scale. Because the unit of analysis was the school, we had two methodologically separate measures of the climate and authenticity for all 87 schools in the sample.

The authenticity scales were drawn from the work of Henderson and Hoy (1982) and Hoy and Henderson (1983). A short version of their Leader Authenticity Scale (LAS) became the model for a Teacher Authenticity Scale (TAS). Items were constructed to capture the aspects of authenticity proposed by Henderson and Hoy—accountability, nonmanipulation, and salience of self over role. Examples of items included the following: "The principal is willing to admit to mistakes when they are made"; "The principal manipulates teachers (reversed)"; "The principal's beliefs and actions are consistent"; "Teachers here manipulate other teachers (reversed)"; and "The teachers' beliefs and actions are consistent."

Factor analysis of the 32 items designed to measure teacher and principal authenticity supported the two separate aspects of authenticity. All 16 items on the Henderson and Hoy LAS were confirmed and remained an independent measure of leader authenticity of the principal. The 16 parallel items written to measure teacher authenticity loaded on a separate factor (teacher authenticity). The reliability coefficients for the two scales were .92 for principal authenticity and .88 for teacher authenticity.

Results

To test each of the hypotheses, two statistical procedures were performed. First, correlations were run between the two openness indices and each aspect of authenticity. Openness indexes were computed by standardizing the scores of the subtests and combining the appropriate subtests (e.g., teacher openness was determined by combining the collegial, committed, and disengaged subtest standard scores). The results were as predicted; openness was related to authenticity. Openness in principal behavior was more strongly related to principal authenticity ($r = .72, p < .01$) than to teacher authenticity ($r = .37, p < .01$). Conversely, openness of teacher behavior was more strongly related to teacher authenticity ($r = .57, p < .01$) than to principal authenticity ($r = .38, p < .01$). Principal openness in principal-teacher relations seems closely associated with perceived authenticity of the principal, whereas teacher openness in behavior is directly linked to perceived teacher authenticity (see Table 2.6).

Next, to get a clearer picture of the openness-authenticity relationships, principal authenticity was regressed on the component elements of principal openness (supportive, directive, and restrictive), and teacher authenticity was regressed on the component elements of teacher openness (collegial, committed, and disengaged). Supportive, directive, and restrictive principal behavior combined to explain 57% of the variance in principal authenticity ($R = .76, p < .01$), with supportive leader behavior the strongest contributor to principal authenticity (see Table 2.7). The data summarized in Table 2.6 also shows that although all components of principal openness are correlated with principal authenticity, it is only supportive principal behavior ($\beta = .61, p < .01$) that makes a unique contribution to the explanation of principal authenticity.

Collegial, committed, and disengaged teacher behavior combined to explain 35% of the variance in teacher authenticity ($R = .61, p < .01$), with collegial teacher behavior the strongest predictor of teacher authenticity. Collegial ($r = .57, p < .01$), committed ($r = .39, p < .01$), and disengaged ($r = -.36, p < .01$) teacher behaviors were all related to teacher authenticity, but only collegial and disengaged teacher behaviors made unique contributions to the explanation of teacher authenticity (see Figure 2.1).

The results of the analysis affirm the hypotheses and support the construct validity of the openness of the climate of middle schools.

A Typology of Middle School Climates

The two general openness dimensions of school climate provide the bases for a typology of school climates arrayed in terms of the

TABLE 2.6 Correlations Among Dimensions of Openness and
             Authenticity

	Principal Authenticity	Teacher Authenticity
Openness of principal	.72**	.37**
Openness of teachers	.38**	.57**

**$p < .01$.

openness of interactions. By cross-partitioning openness in principal
behavior with openness in teacher behavior, four categories of
climate are defined (see Table 2.8). These climate types are similar to
those found in elementary schools (Hoy & Clover, 1986).

Open Climate

The open climate is one in which the principal is supportive of
the teachers' actions and suggestions; the principal gives freedom to
teachers to act and does not supervise closely; and the principal
avoids "bureaucratic trivia," not burdening or hindering teachers
with busywork. The faculty in an open climate respects the professional competence of their colleagues, has warm and open feelings
for fellow teachers, is open to students and committed to helping
them, and is neither critical of others nor disruptive. In brief, both the
teachers and the principal are open in their behaviors.

Engaged Climate

The engaged climate is one in which the teachers work together
to accomplish their goals, they are committed to their students, and
they cooperate with each other. The principal, on the other hand,
does not support the teachers in their actions, closely supervises
their performance, and does not shield the staff from the burdens of
bureaucratic routine. Nevertheless, the faculty members work
together as professionals, in spite of, not because of the principal.
The faculty is engaged in the professional work of the school, dedicated to their students, and respectful of each other. In short, although teacher-principal relations are closed, the faculty has open
interactions with both their students and colleagues.

TABLE 2.7 Regression of Aspects of Authenticity on Dimensions of Climate Openness

| | Aspects of Authenticity | | | |
| | Principal Authenticity | | Teacher Authenticity | |
Dimensions of Organizational Climate	r	Beta	r	Beta
Principal behavior				
Supportive	.74**	.61**		
Directive	−.50**	−.09		
Restrictive	−.48**	−.17		
	$R = .76$**	Adjusted $R^2 = .57$		
Teacher behavior				
Collegial			.57**	.49**
Committed			.39**	.05
Disengaged			−.36**	−.22*
			$R = .61$**	
				Adjusted $R^2 = .35$

**p < .01.

Disengaged Climate

The disengaged climate is the opposite of the engaged climate. The principal supports the teachers, gives them the professional courtesy to do what is necessary, is open to constructive suggestions, and attempts to keep the bureaucratic impediments at a minimum. Faculty members, however, are indifferent to each other and the principal. Moreover, they do not go out of their way to help students and they are prone to sabotage actions of peers as well as those of the principal. The faculty does not like the principal, and teachers are disengaged from the tasks at hand. In brief, although the principal's behavior is open, teacher behaviors are closed.

Closed Climate

Schools with a closed climate are not pleasant places for the principal, the faculty, or the students. The principal distrusts the actions and motives of faculty, does not support teachers, is rigid and

Principal Openness

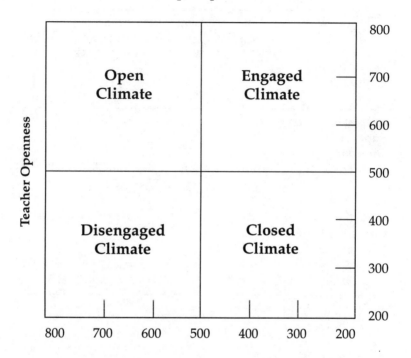

Figure 2.1. Typology of Middle School Climates

authoritarian, and is perceived as burying the faculty in needless paperwork. Principal behavior is controlling. The faculty in a closed climate is apathetic, self-involved, uncaring about students as well as one another, and unwilling to accept responsibility. In brief, both principal and teacher behaviors are guarded and closed.

Summary and Discussion

The OCDQ-RM is a 50-item climate instrument with six dimensions that describe the behavior of middle school teachers and principals. This instrument, unlike other versions of the OCDQ, was designed for use in middle schools. It measures three aspects of principal behavior—supportive, directive, and restrictive—and three aspects of teacher behavior—collegial, committed, and disengaged. These six aspects of interactions define two openness dimensions of middle school climate—the openness of teacher-principal relations and the openness of teacher-teacher and student-teacher relations.

Open principal behavior is reflected in authentic relations with teachers. The principal creates an environment that is supportive; encourages teacher autonomy; and frees teachers from routine, busywork so they can concentrate on teaching. The principal is open and approachable to teachers and genuinely concerned with their social needs as well as the task achievement of the school. In contrast, closed principal behavior is rigid, close, and nonsupportive.

Open teacher behavior is also expressed in authentic interactions, especially with colleagues and students. Teachers are open and professional in their interactions with each other as well as their students. Teacher behavior is sincere, positive, friendly, and constructive. There is a functional flexibility in both open principal and open teacher behavior. These two general dimensions of climate openness define four climate types—Open, Engaged, Disengaged, and Closed.

Both dimensions of openness were related to independent measures of authenticity. Open principals were seen as authentic in their interactions with teachers. Likewise, open teacher behavior was perceived as more authentic than closed teacher behavior. Although both dimensions of openness were related to both aspects of authenticity, as predicted, openness of principal behavior was more strongly related to perceptions of principal authenticity, whereas openness of teacher behavior was more strongly related to perceptions of teacher authenticity. Any influence of principal behavior on openness and authenticity is more directly tied to principal-teacher interactions than to teacher-teacher or teacher-student relations.

The psychometric properties of the six subtests of the OCDQ-RM are strong. All the scales have high reliability coefficients. The subtests are reasonably pure; the factor matrices demonstrate that items load high on one subtest and low on the others. The factor structure is stable; it was similar for two separate samples. The empirical results also provide strong construct-related evidence for the validity of principal and teacher openness as pivotal dimensions of school climate.

The original rationale for creating the OCDQ-RM was that middle schools were different than either elementary or secondary schools; thus, a separate climate instrument for the middle school was necessary. The results of this research support that decision. Middle schools are indeed different; not surprisingly, they are a cross between elementary and high schools. On one hand, middle schools have the collegial and disengaged relations of teachers in elementary schools, but they lack the intimacy found in both elementary and secondary schools; that is, intimacy is not a dimension of middle school climate. Similarly, as in elementary schools, middle school climate does not have a teacher frustration dimension. On the other hand, middle schools have a commitment dimension that resembles the engagement dimension found in high schools but with a greater emphasis on commitment to students rather than to the school or colleagues. Middle schools have the same three aspects of principal leadership (supportive, directive, restrictive) as elementary schools, but even here the subtests are measured with slightly different items that are more appropriate for the middle school. In brief, middle school climate resembles elementary more than secondary school climate, but even here the differences are great enough to warrant a separate measure of organizational climate for middle schools.

Implications

The constructs of school climate and openness have theoretical, research, and practical implications. Whether one's focus is theory or research or the practice of administration, the development of the OCDQ-RM opens up a host of opportunities.

Theory and Research

Open and authentic interactions in schools should be goals in themselves. Not only are they worthy ends that are indispensable to healthy organizational dynamics but they are likely means to many positive school outcomes. Schools should be places where teachers and students want to be rather than have to be. Open and authentic relations move the school in that direction. We suspect that schools with open climates are places where students feel better about themselves and their teachers and where trust among students, teachers, and administrators is high.

One key to successful leadership is to lead by example (Bennis, 1989; Hoy et al., 1991; Pelz, 1952). In middle schools, the principal who leads by example—that is, who does not ask teachers to do anything that he or she would not do and is supportive and helpful with teachers—will likely find voluntary compliance and cooperation among teachers. This does not mean the principals will not criticize, but when criticism comes it will be constructive. Rigid, domineering principal behavior rarely produces commitment; to the contrary, in an atmosphere of close monitoring and suspicion, teachers will likely become alienated, uncooperative, and turn against each other and the principal. Leadership that is supportive, encourages teacher initiation, and frees teachers from administrative trivia is instrumental in forging an open organizational climate. Moreover, open relations between teachers and principals are necessary if schools are to become truly professional organizations. Some researchers (Hoy & Forsyth, 1986; Sergiovanni, 1992) have argued that effective supervision is only possible when relationships between supervisors and teachers are open, collegial, and nonthreatening. The notion of openness seems critical for long-term productive relationships among colleagues and between superiors and subordinates.

The one distinct concept that emerged in the study of middle school climate was commitment: teacher commitment to students, not commitment to the school or colleagues. Although commitment to clients is a central property of professionalism (Blau & Scott, 1961; Hoy & Miskel, 1991), organizational researchers do not study it as frequently as either commitment to colleagues or commitment to the organization (Mowday, Steers, & Porter, 1979; Rosenholtz, 1989; Tarter, Bliss, & Hoy, 1989). Commitment to students requires more research both to refine its conceptual underpinnings and to explore its relationships with such student outcome variables as achievement, self-efficacy, and self-esteem.

The OCDQ-RM is a heuristic research tool; it suggests many important research questions. For example, to what extent does openness in teacher behavior affect such student outcomes as self-concept, commitment to school, motivation, absenteeism, vandalism, and student achievement? What are the antecedents to open principal behavior? When and how can principals move to a more open style? No one leadership style, not even an open one, is successful in all situations. Under what conditions does open principal behavior create open teacher interactions, healthy interpersonal relationships, trust, and a commitment to teaching and helping students? Although structural changes are relatively easy to make, they often have little impact on students or the functioning of schools (Cuban, 1992; Mergendoller, 1993). To what extent do structural changes in middle schools affect the climate? What kind of structural changes are related to more open school relationships? The typology of school climate developed in this research is a framework for the study of leadership, motivation, organizational communication, school structure, decision making, goal setting, discipline, and control. These examples are only a glimpse of the important issues to be addressed.

Finally, we predict that openness of school climate will be related to other measures that are indicators of quality middle schools such as student achievement, organizational effectiveness, innovativeness, flexibility, and strong and cohesive school cultures. We will, in fact, explore the relationship between these and other quality indicators in Chapter 4.

Practice

The climate framework and its measures also underscore a number of more immediate and practical implications. Administrators can use the OCDQ-RM as an organizing framework, as a diagnostic tool, and as a guide to action. Many principals informally classify what happens in a school in terms of how well they are getting the job done or how teachers feel about their initiatives. The climate framework provides a perspective for principals to reflect about how they are doing. How open are their relationships with teachers? How open are teachers with each other? How committed are teachers to helping students achieve? How disengaged are teachers? In short, the climate framework itself is an organizational and conceptual guide for administrator self-reflection and analysis.

The OCDQ-RM can also be used in a more formal way. It is easy to administer to faculty, easy to score, and easy to interpret; in fact, using the norms developed in the current study it is possible to identify a school as one of four climate types—open, engaged, disengaged, closed (see Chapter 5). Thus, the instrument can be used as a diagnostic device. Our experiences with nearly 100 faculties convince us that teachers do not mind, in fact rather enjoy, responding to the OCDQ-RM. Ten minutes of a faculty meeting and it's done.

The instrument not only identifies those schools that are closed or open but it pinpoints those aspects of school climate that are undesirable and in need of amelioration. For example, lack of openness in principal-teacher relations may be a function of teachers' perceptions that the principal is restrictive, that is, burdens teachers with busywork. The principal may be surprised and think the teachers are wrong. It really doesn't matter who is right or wrong; the principal has a problem—the teachers have a perception of restrictiveness. The principal should get to the bottom of the perception. Indeed, one fascinating outcome of a climate analysis is the discovery of discrepancies when the principal compares his or her perceptions of the climate with those of the faculty. This is a good "reality check." Clearly, the instrument describes teacher-teacher and teacher-principal relations in a more systematic way than personal impressions of the administrator.

Finally, the OCDQ-RM can be used for inservice and professional development for both teachers and administrators. The profile of school climate is a snapshot of the school at a given point in time. The picture does not explain why things are the way they are—it merely describes what exists. Teachers and administrators who find their schools in need of change must begin to uncover the causes of the existing climate. Once the causes have been diagnosed, then strategies for planned change can be implemented. Successive administrations of the OCDQ-RM can roughly gauge the success of the improvement interventions.

In the final chapter of this book, we will describe how the OCDQ-RM can be used in a systematic way to assess and improve schools. Details on administering, scoring, and interpreting the information will be given in a step-by-step fashion. Concrete examples will be provided and strategies for using the information to change school climate will be described and illustrated. Some administrators, particularly superintendents, might be tempted to use the instrument for school evaluation. Don't do it. This practice will inevitably diminish the usefulness of the measure in self-improvement and organizational development.

In the next chapter we turn to another perspective on organizational climate; we explore the health of school climates rather than their openness. The health perspective provides a different but complementary view of the dynamics of school life.

Notes

1. This chapter draws heavily from Hoy, Hoffman, Sabo, and Bliss (1996).

2. There has been a recent shift in the meaning of validity. Validity is now seen as a unitary concept based on various forms of evidence—content-related, criterion-related, and construct-related evidence. For instructive discussions on this shift see Cronbach (1989), Gronlund (1993), Messick (1989), and Moss (1992).

CHAPTER

3

THE ORGANIZATIONAL HEALTH INVENTORY FOR MIDDLE SCHOOLS

A reasonably clear conception of organizational health would seem to be an important prerequisite to a wide range of activities involving organizations: research of any meaningful sort; attempts to improve the organization as a place to live, work, and learn; and—not the least—the day-to-day operation of any particular organization, such as your own school system.

Matthew Miles, 1969,
Planned Change and Organizational Health

In the last chapter we looked at the climate of middle schools using the notion of "personality." We developed and tested an instrument, the OCDQ-RM, to assess the openness of middle school climates. In this chapter, we use a different vantage point to explore and assess the climate of a school. Here the focus is on the health of the organization.

53

School health also refers to the organizational climate of schools, but it describes the vitality and dynamics of professional interactions of students, teachers, and administrators. The health of elementary and secondary schools has been conceptualized, operationalized, and tested in numerous studies (Hoy & Barnes, 1997; Hoy & Tarter, 1997a, 1997b; Hoy, Tarter, & Kottkamp, 1991; Tarter & Hoy, 1988). That research has demonstrated the utility of the health framework for the study and improvement of elementary and secondary schools, but middle schools are different than either elementary or junior or senior high schools. Is the middle school more like an elementary or secondary school? That is a good question because the middle school has trappings of both. It is also an empirical question. We now examine these questions. To be more specific, the purposes of this chapter are first, to conceptualize and develop an organizational health inventory for middle schools (OHI-M); then, to compare the aspects of school health among elementary, middle, and high schools; and finally, to assess the validity of the construct by testing several theoretically derived hypotheses.

Developing a New School Health Measure: The OHI-M

The development of a health measure for middle schools had five phases:

- Conceptualizing school health
- Generating items to operationalize the construct
- Conducting a pilot study to reduce and refine items and dimensions of school health
- Conducting a second study to test the stability of the factor structure of the construct
- Testing the reliability of the new middle school instrument (OHI-M)

Conceptual Framework

The organizational health of a school describes the interpersonal dynamics of students, teachers, and administrators in a school; it is one conception of the school climate. We have defined organizational climate as a set of internal characteristics that distinguishes one school from another and influences the behavior of its members. In more specific terms, school climate is the relatively stable property of the school environment that is experienced by participants, affects their behavior, and is based on their collective perceptions of behavior in schools (Hoy & Miskel, 1991; Taguiri, 1968).

The impetus for using the metaphor of health and well-being to examine the climate of schools came from Miles' (1969) early work. Healthy organizations not only survive in their environments over the short run but continue to extend their abilities and progress over the long haul. The theoretical framework for the organizational health of middle schools was based on the work of Parsons, Bales, and Shils (1953) and Hoy and his colleagues (Hoy & Clover, 1986; Hoy & Feldman, 1987; Hoy et al., 1991). All social systems, including schools, must solve four basic problems if they are to survive, grow, and be effective. Each must accommodate to its environment, set and implement its goals, maintain a cohesive system, and create and preserve a distinctive culture (Parsons et al., 1953). In brief, healthy schools adapt to their environments, achieve their goals, and infuse common values and solidarity into the teacher work group.

Parsons (1967) explains that schools have three distinct levels of control over activities as they attempt to solve their basic problems and meet their needs—the technical, managerial, and institutional.

- The *technical level* is concerned with the primary mission of the school—teaching and learning. Teachers and supervisors have the primary responsibility of solving the problems associated with teaching and learning.

- The *managerial level* controls the internal coordination of the school. Principals must allocate resources and coordinate the work effort; they must find ways to develop teacher loyalty, trust, and commitment, and to motivate teachers.

- Finally, the *institutional level* connects the school and the community. Schools need the support of their communities. Both teachers and administrators need backing if they are to perform their respective functions in a harmonious fashion without undue pressure from individuals and groups outside the school.

This broad Parsonian perspective provided the theoretical underpinnings for defining and measuring school health. A healthy middle school is one in which the technical, managerial, and institutional levels are in harmony and the school is meeting its basic needs as it successfully copes with disruptive external forces and directs its energies toward its mission. In healthy schools, students, teachers, administrators, and the community work together cooperatively and constructively.

In more specific terms, seven dimensions of school health were conceptualized based on the earlier work of Hoy and his colleagues (Hoy & Clover, 1986; Hoy & Feldman, 1987; Hoy et al., 1991). The dimensions were selected to represent each of the basic needs of social systems as well as the three levels of control found in most organizations. The levels and dimensions are briefly summarized next.

Technical Level

Morale is a collective sense of friendliness, openness, enthusiasm, and trust among faculty members. Teachers like each other, like their jobs, and help each other; they are proud of their school and have a sense of accomplishment.

Academic emphasis is the extent to which the school is driven for academic excellence. High but achievable academic goals are set for students; the learning environment is serious and orderly; teachers believe in the ability of their students to achieve; and students work hard and admire and respect those who are high achievers.

Managerial Level

Principal influence is the principal's ability to influence the actions of superiors. Being able to influence superiors, to get additional resources, and independence are important administrative attributes.

Consideration is principal behavior that is friendly, supportive, open, and collegial—a genuine concern by the principal for the welfare of the teachers.

Initiating structure is principal behavior that is both task and achievement oriented. Work expectations, standards of performance, and procedures are articulated clearly by the principal.

Resource support is the degree to which teachers have adequate supplies and instructional materials and can readily get additional resources if they request them.

Institutional Level

Institutional integrity is the school's ability to cope with its environment in a way that maintains the educational integrity of its programs. Teachers are protected from unreasonable community and parental demands.

In sum, healthy schools have strong academic programs that are protected from unreasonable outside demands (institutional integrity). They have administrators who have influence with their superiors (principal influence), are able to get additional resources for their teachers (resource support), and are achievement orientated (initiating structure), as well as supportive and collegial (consideration). Finally, teachers in the school are open, friendly, and committed (morale), and have created a strong academic learning environment that is serious, orderly, and efficacious (academic emphasis).

Measuring School Health

Once we decided to use the theoretical foundations of Parsons to develop and refine the notion of organizational health, a strategy to generate items became clear. Rather than reinventing the construct and its measure, we built on the work of Hoy and his colleagues (Hoy & Clover, 1986; Hoy & Feldman, 1987; Hoy et al., 1991). We started by using all the items that were on the organizational health inventories for elementary (OHI-M) and secondary (OHI) schools. In effect, an empirical test was used to see which items from each instrument worked for middle schools. Next, we wrote an additional 16 items designed to capture distinct properties of middle schools. Items were developed by the researchers independently and jointly, but no items were included on the initial instrument unless there was agreement on the following criteria:

- Each item represented an aspect of a middle school.
- Each statement was clear and concise.
- Each statement had content validity.
- Each statement measured one of the climate dimensions.

In all, 72 Likert-type items were used in the preliminary version of the health inventory for middle schools: 17 items that were unique

to the secondary version; 9 items that were unique to the elementary
version; 28 items that were common to both elementary and secondary versions; and 18 new items that were written specifically for middle schools. Examples of items added included the following: "The
principal eats with the teachers"; "Teachers inform parents about
their concerns about students"; and "Students select teachers to discuss their personal concerns." Teachers were asked to indicate the
extent to which each statement characterized their school along a
4-point scale from *rarely occurs, sometimes occurs, often occurs,* to *very
frequently occurs.*

Pilot Study

To examine the factor structure of the new middle school instrument, the OHI-M, a small pilot study was conducted. Eighty-six
teachers from 86 different middle schools responded to the 72-item
preliminary questionnaire. The sample of schools represented a
diverse set of middle schools in terms of size, socioeconomic status,
and ethnicity within New Jersey. The items on the instrument represented the basic dimensions of school health—institutional integrity,
principal influence, initiating structure, consideration, resource support, morale, and academic emphasis.

A series of exploratory factor analyses of the pilot data was performed, anticipating a seven-factor solution. A six-factor solution,
however, emerged as the best solution using a principal components
factor analysis with a varimax rotation. The following criteria were
used to assess the results and refine the measure:

- Simple structure—items load high on one factor and near zero
  on the others.
- Conceptual fit—items are theoretically consistent with each
  other.
- Substantial factor loadings—items had factor loadings of
  greater than .45.

Using these criteria, 23 of the 72 items were eliminated; that is, those
items that did not load strongly on one and only one factor, had weak
factor loadings, or did not fit conceptually were deleted.

In the final factor analysis of the pilot study, the remaining 49 items defined 6 factors that were named Institutional Integrity, Principal Influence, Resource Support, Collegial Leadership, Academic Emphasis, and Teacher Affiliation. The six factors accounted for 76.2% of all the variance. Two of the items of the instrument were conceptually ambiguous and 2 were mistakenly repeated; thus, these 4 items were eliminated, which left 45 items measuring 6 elements of middle school health. Two of the predicted dimensions of the construct of health merged into one; initiating structure and consideration items defined the same factor, which we called Collegial Leadership. The morale items came together with other items describing the expressive relationships among the faculty; hence, we renamed this aspect of health Teacher Affiliation. Reliabilities of all six scales were high (see Table 3.1).

In sum, six factors were identified. The subtests for each factor had high reliabilities. Thus, we had a 45-item health instrument for middle schools ready for further testing and analysis—an instrument that we labeled the Organizational Health Inventory for Middle Schools (OHI-M).

A Further Test of the Middle School Instrument (OHI-M)

After the pilot analysis and refinement of the instrument, the revised 45-item OHI-M was ready to be tested with a new and more comprehensive set of data. Eighty-six middle schools were selected to demonstrate the stability of the factor structure, and to confirm the validity and stability of the subtests.

Sample

The unit of analysis was the school because climate variables reflect organizational properties (Hoy et al., 1991; Sirotnik, 1980). A new sample of 86 middle schools, which included responses from 2,741 teachers, was drawn. Although it was not possible to select a random sample of New Jersey middle schools, care was taken to select urban, suburban, and rural schools from diverse geographic areas of the state as well as from all socioeconomic levels in the state. Only middle schools that had a 5-8, 6-8, or 7-8 configuration were included in the sample. Small middle schools, those with fewer than

TABLE 3.1 Reliabilities of the Six Scales

	Number of Items	Reliability (alpha)
Academic Emphasis	9	.92
Teacher Affiliation	8	.90
Collegial Leadership	9	.92
Principal Influence	6	.82
Resource Support	6	.90
Institutional Integrity	7	.88
Total items	45	

15 teachers, were not included. Using the state's measure of socioeconomic status, 28% of the schools came from the lowest levels, 37% came from the middle levels, and 35% came from the highest levels. Fifteen of the 21 counties in New Jersey were represented in the sample.

Data Collection

Data were collected from teachers at regularly scheduled faculty meetings, at which time the purpose of the study was explained in general terms, anonymity was guaranteed, and the importance of candid responses was emphasized. Teachers at the meeting were divided into three random groups, with one group responding to the OHI-M, a second group describing school climate (OCDQ-M), and a third group responding to a set of scales that mapped other organizational properties. This procedure was used because the unit of analysis was the school (data were aggregated at the school level) and because it ensured methodological separation of the independent and dependent variables. Virtually everyone in attendance responded to the instruments.

Factor Analysis

School mean scores were calculated for each item of the climate instrument, and the item-correlation matrix for the 86 schools was factor analyzed. A principal components factor analysis with a varimax rotation confirmed the six predicted health dimensions; in fact, the results were virtually identical to those found in the pilot study. The final version of the OHI-M contained 45 items that defined 6 factors of school health; their eigenvalues ranged from 1.90 to 16.07 explaining 77.20% of the variance (see Table 3.2).

The results demonstrated the stability of the factor structure found in the pilot study; all of the factors were replicated. Academic Emphasis and Teacher Affiliation depicted teacher-teacher and teacher-student relationships; Principal Influence, Collegial Leadership, and Resource Support described the leadership of the principal; and Institutional Integrity captured the degree to which teachers perceived they were protected from hostile forces in the community. The alpha coefficients of reliability for all six subtests were high: Academic Emphasis (.94), Teacher Affiliation (.94), Principal Influence (.94), Collegial Leadership (.94), Resource Support (.96), and Institutional Integrity (.93). A comparison of these findings with the pilot results (see Table 3.1) demonstrated that the six dimensions are identical and the reliability of the subtests on the final form are slightly higher. Constitutive definitions and sample items for each dimension of health are provided in Table 3.3.

The stability of the factor structure also provides construct-related evidence for the six dimensions of health. Factor analysis enables the researcher to study the theoretical meanings of constructs. In the current study, six hypothetical dimensions of school health were postulated and then empirically demonstrated. The relations among the items measuring each health dimension were systematically related to each other, as expected, in the factor analysis of the OHI-M. The strong loadings in the predicted six-factor solution as well as the high reliabilities of the subtests suggest that the OHI-M is a useful instrument with high reliability and substantial validity.

Second-Order Factor Analysis

Thus far, we have been concerned with identifying items that formed the six basic dimensions of middle school health. Halpin and Croft (1962) propose three standards for evaluating a battery of tests. First, each subtest should measure relatively different types of behavior. An examination of the correlation matrix among the six subtests (see Table 3.4) demonstrates our success on this standard; most intercorrelations among the measures were weak to moderate.

TABLE 3.2 Varimax Rotated Factor Matrix: Analysis of OHI-M
(N = 86)

Item	Factor I	Factor II	Factor III	Factor IV	Factor V	Factor VI
01	.12685	*.83331*	.14093	.20058	.15693	.12482
02	*.77106*	.14258	.13282	.08166	.07959	.13776
03	.15778	−.08314	−.03193	*.74403*	.26075	.34216
04	.12685	*.66526*	.25420	.33239	.10998	.08556
05	.21503	*.88356*	.13006	.13716	.01738	.07861
06	.27016	.29281	.17766	.16145	.19335	*.73098*
07	*.83007*	−.06376	−.01568	.06793	−.04107	.19054
08	.11882	.23416	.15877	.05296	*.72695*	.25983
09	.19983	.13148	.07430	*.72593*	.18727	.09693
10	.13324	*.84428*	.17669	−.05042	.12353	.09871
11	.37299	.16366	.18313	.14875	.03597	*.84221*
12	.11235	.15956	*.88852*	.07806	.09070	.08809
13	−.13150	.13983	−.08999	.02574	*.85467*	.02781
14	−.08668	*.49620*	.33116	.29742	.27421	−.15915
15	.39326	.16388	.21885	.11559	.11335	*.80478*
16	*.86810*	.12648	.16350	.01604	−.05177	.21811
17	*.87718*	.11850	.03016	.04120	.18644	.22463
18	.28253	.09984	.01239	.01794	*.86696*	.06461
19	.24281	.18456	.00767	*.83986*	.05909	.14247
20	.38196	.07673	.19305	.25348	.18456	*.76266*
21	.17000	.14838	*.87355*	.07951	.02637	.17665
22	*.81352*	.14109	.02990	.13608	.05425	.10482
23	.02259	.02311	.04995	.08206	*.86675*	.09611
24	.16316	*.82070*	.13938	.09402	.13736	.14151
25	.09640	.07904	.05100	.17491	*.90478*	.06821

Second, the battery as a whole should tap enough common behavior to permit researchers to find a pattern of more general factors. And third, the general factors extracted should not be discordant with those already reported in the literature. We now turn to the latter two standards.

Based on the extant literature (Hoy et al., 1991), we postulated a general dimension of health undergirding middle school climate. A second-order factor analysis of the six subtests of the OHI-M was therefore performed on the subtest correlation matrix. The theoretical and empirical questions guiding the second-order factor analysis were the following:

TABLE 3.2 Continued

Item	Factor I	Factor II	Factor III	Factor IV	Factor V	Factor VI
26	.07788	.16143	.00343	.13448	*.88089*	.02735
27	*.83441*	.19130	.14531	.10855	.09063	.19086
28	.51069	.18833	*.52953*	.16963	.09916	.22705
29	*.65399*	.29959	.40169	.04965	.03738	.22066
30	.15850	*.86146*	.17990	.02626	.03559	.17722
31	.32627	.35372	*.60176*	.04417	.18493	.12505
32	.18712	.12381	*.78126*	.17541	.03936	.11413
33	.20716	.33805	.15244	.10648	*.65813*	.13991
34	.03843	.17981	.11607	*.89351*	.04796	.06749
35	.07082	*.83548*	.15129	.15152	.13507	.09629
36	.40640	.29441	.27455	.10851	.11533	*.72859*
37	.08862	.08891	*.75132*	.21061	.05882	.21443
38	*.57813*	.13125	.30002	.23741	−.07271	.31925
39	.08394	*.74992*	.08550	.02108	−.02712	.39863
40	.25238	.22959	.10955	.21788	.05258	*.79149*
41	.00662	−.02506	.14695	*.80684*	−.01025	.01632
42	.09684	.20040	*.85892*	.01586	.00524	.08994
43	.09398	.15579	.19748	*.85313*	.11613	.16527
44	*.74833*	.09619	.22191	.09785	.09596	.17514
45	.06818	.19380	*.87239*	.01207	.08813	.04945
Eigenvalue	16.07	6.25	4.38	3.67	3.25	1.90
Percentage of cumulative variance	34.9	48.5	58.1	66.0	73.1	77.2

NOTE: Italicized numbers represent the defining factor loadings.

- Is there a general factor of organizational health underlying middle school health?
- If so, is such a health factor consistent with the notions of health that have been described in the literature (Hoy & Feldman, 1987; Hoy et al., 1991)?

A factor analysis of the correlation matrix for the six subtests did produce a general dimension of school health. The one-factor solution with a varimax rotation is given in Table 3.5. Consistent with earlier findings, all six factors loaded on the first factor, which we called General School Health.

TABLE 3.3 Dimensions of School Health: Definitions and Sample Items

Dimension	Definition	Sample Items
Academic emphasis	The extent to which the school is driven by a quest for excellence. High but achievable goals are set for students; the learning environment is orderly and serious; and students work hard and respect those who do well academically.	• The learning environment is orderly and serious. • Students respect others who get good grades. • Students try hard to improve on previous work. • Students neglect to complete homework.*
Teacher affiliation	Refers to a general friendliness in the school and a strong affiliation with the school. Teachers feel good about each other, their job, and their students.	• Teachers exhibit friendliness to each other. • Teachers accomplish their jobs with enthusiasm. • Teachers do favors for each other. • Teachers are indifferent to each other.*
Collegial leadership	Refers to principal behavior that is friendly, supportive, open, and guided by norms of equality. The principal sets the tone for high performance.	• The principal is friendly and approachable. • The principal is willing to make changes. • The principal lets faculty know what is expected of them.

Principal influence	Refers to the principal's ability to affect the action of superiors. The principal is persuasive with and works effectively with superiors.	• The principal gets what he or she asks for from superiors. • The principal is able to work well with the superintendent. • The principal is rebuffed by the superintendent.*
Resource support	Refers primarily to classroom supplies and instructional materials. They are readily available; indeed, extra materials are easily obtained.	• Teachers receive necessary classroom supplies. • Extra materials are available if requested. • Our school gets its fair share of resources from the district.
Institutional integrity	The degree to which a school can cope with its environment in a way that maintains the educational integrity of its programs. Teachers are protected from unreasonable community demands.	• The school is open to the whims of the public.* • Select citizen groups are influential with the board.* • Teachers are protected from unreasonable community and parental demands.

* = scored in reverse.

65

TABLE 3.4 Intercorrelations of the Six Subtests of the OHI-M

Subtest	1	2	3	4	5	6
1. Academic Emphasis	(.94)[a]					
2. Teacher Affiliation	.48	(.94)				
3. Collegial Leadership	.32	.49	(.94)			
4. Principal Influence	.26	.28	.31	(.94)		
5. Resource Support	.61	.52	.46	.39	(.96)	
6. Institutional Integrity	−.09	.09	.26	.21	.21	(.93)

a. Alpha coefficients of reliability are reported in the parentheses.

Factor I, General School Health, is characterized by teacher and student behavior that is healthy. Teachers like their colleagues, their school, their job, and their students (teacher affiliation), and they are driven by a quest for academic excellence. Teachers believe in themselves and their students; consequently, they set high but achievable goals. The learning environment is serious and orderly, and students work hard and respect others who do well academically (academic emphasis).

Principal behavior is also healthy; that is, friendly, open, egalitarian, supportive, as well as expecting the best from teachers (collegial leadership). Principals get teachers the resources they need to do the job (resource support) and are also influential with superiors (principal influence); they go to bat for their teachers. Finally, a healthy school has institutional integrity; that is, teachers are protected from unreasonable and hostile outside forces. This profile of school health is indicated by a single, general factor of school health. An index of school health can be computed by summing the standardized scores for all the health dimensions. The formula for the index is found in Chapter 5.

Organizational Health and Faculty Trust: Some Hypotheses and a Test

The next step in the study was to construct some hypotheses using the notions of health and trust. A consistent feature in the literature on leadership and organizations has been the importance

TABLE 3.5 Second-Order Factor Analysis of OHI-M

	Factor I
1. Academic Emphasis	.712
2. Teacher Affiliation	.763
3. Collegial Leadership	.716
4. Principal Influence	.590
5. Resource Support	.841
6. Institutional Integrity	.282
Eigenvalue	2.735
Variance	45.6

of trust in developing productive social relations. Three decades ago, Likert (1967) identified trust as a critical element in the interaction-influence process of organizational life. More recently, Sergiovanni (1991) has argued that trust is indispensable to moral leadership. Other contemporary organizational scholars (Bennis, 1989; Ouchi, 1981) have similarly concluded that trust is a fundamental feature of successful superior-subordinate relationships in organizational life.

Faculty Trust

As common as the concept of trust is, it is also ambiguous. Indeed, there are almost as many conceptions of trust as there are commentaries about it. Typically, the reader in education finds only general discussions of trust. Principals admonish their teachers to trust them, teachers search for trustworthy colleagues, and commentators extol the virtues of trust. There is little doubt that trust is a popular concept, but there is also little systematic analysis of trust; in fact, research on faculty trust in schools is rare. Because our analysis is an empirical examination of faculty trust in schools, it is important to clearly define the dimensions of trust that are of concern. Drawing on the work of Rotter (1967), Golembiewski and McConkie (1975), and Hoy and Kupersmith (1985), we define faculty trust first conceptually, and then operationally.

Trust is a general confidence and overall optimism in occurring events: It is believing in others in the absence of compelling reasons to disbelieve. In the context of organizations, *trust is a work group's generalized expectancy that the words, actions, and promises of another individual, group, or organization can be relied on* (Hoy & Kupersmith, 1985). Hence, in a school setting, trust can be examined from a variety of reference groups—students, teachers, or administrators. Individuals trust others, not only to be consistent in action, but to act with good intentions. In the current analysis, we are concerned with faculty trust as it is expressed toward the principal and fellow teachers. In particular, two aspects of faculty trust are the foci for this inquiry:

- *Trust in the Principal.* The faculty has confidence that the principal will keep his or her word and act in the best interest of teachers.

- *Trust in Colleagues.* The faculty believes that teachers can depend on each other in difficult situations and that teachers can rely on the integrity of their colleagues.

Faculty Trust and Organization Health

Faculty trust and school health should complement each other. Healthy interpersonal relationships should promote trust among teachers and between teachers and administrators. Conversely, trust should facilitate the development of healthy organizational interactions. Hence, the trust-health relationships are ones of mutual dependence and reciprocal influence; that is, healthy organizations promote trust and trust produces healthy organizations. There is empirical evidence to support such relationships in elementary schools (Hoy, Tarter, & Wiskoskie, 1992) and in high schools (Tarter & Hoy, 1988), but not so for middle schools. The theory for the connection is consistent regardless of school level.

Trust is an intrinsic element in the development of cohesive relationships in organizations (Parsons, 1961); in fact, trust is a important element in the development of social integration and openness in school climate (Hoffman, Sabo, Bliss, & Hoy, 1994). Moreover, as the culture of the school becomes more cohesive, it becomes more open (see Chapter 4) and trust is reinforced (Hoffman et al., 1994). Finally, there is empirical evidence linking openness and faculty trust (Hoffman et al., 1994). Moreover, open interpersonal relations tend to be healthy ones (Hannum, 1994). To examine the trust-health relationship in middle schools as well as to assess the construct-related validity of our notion of organizational health, we tested the following two hypotheses:

H1   The healthier the organizational climate of middle schools, the greater the degree of faculty trust in the principal.

H2   The healthier the organizational climate of middle schools, the greater the degree of faculty trust in colleagues.

Faculty Trust Scales

We turn to the operational definitions of two aspects of faculty trust. Measures were first developed by Hoy and Kupersmith (1985) to gauge faculty trust in the principal and in colleagues for high schools. The same dimensions of trust were replicated for middle schools in a factor-analytic study by Hoffman et al. (1994). Teachers were asked to describe their interpersonal relations and feelings along a 6-point Likert scale from *strongly disagree* to *strongly agree*. Sample items for each dimension were as follows:

Trust in the Principal
- The principal in this school keeps his or her word.
- The principal in this school takes unfair advantage of teachers (score reversed).

Trust in Colleagues
- Even in difficult situations teachers in this school can depend on one another.
- Teachers in this school are suspicious of each other (score reversed).

The two trust measures were each composed of seven items. Both scales are highly reliable with alpha coefficients of reliability in the current study at .86 for faculty trust in the principal and .91 for faculty trust in colleagues. The evidence for construct validity of the scales is supported by two factor-analytic studies (Hoffman et al., 1994; Hoy & Kupersmith, 1985).

Results

To test each of the hypotheses, two statistical procedures were performed. First, correlations were computed between the general health index and each aspect of trust. The general health index was determined by standardizing the scores for each of the six subtests and then summing and averaging them. The results were as predicted; the overall health of the middle school was significantly related to both aspects of faculty trust. Faculty trust in the principal was strongly related to school health ($r = .64, p < .01$), whereas faculty trust in colleagues was moderately related to school health ($r = .36, p < .01$). In general, the healthier the organizational climate of middle schools, the greater the degree of faculty trust. The zero-order correlations between each component of health and each aspect of faculty trust also support the hypotheses (see Table 3.6).

Next, to get a clearer picture of the trust-health relationships, each aspect of faculty trust was regressed on all the component elements of school health (academic emphasis, teacher affiliation, collegial leadership, principal influence, resource support, and institutional integrity). These elements combined to explain 68% of the variance in faculty trust in the principal ($R = .82, p < .01$), with collegial leader behavior the strongest contributor to faculty trust in the principal (see Table 3.7). The data summarized in Table 3.7 also show that, except for institutional integrity, all of the components of school health are correlated with faculty trust in the principal; however, only collegial leadership (beta = .73, $p < .01$) and teacher affiliation (beta = .17, $p < .05$) make unique contributions to the explanation of faculty trust.

The elements of school health combined to explain 44% of the variance in faculty trust in colleagues ($R = .66, p < .01$), with teacher affiliation the strongest predictor of trust in colleagues. Again, most of the elements of school health are related to faculty trust in colleagues. Principal influence is a noteworthy exception; the influence of the principal apparently does not help generate trust among colleagues (see Table 3.7). The results of the analysis, however, affirm the hypotheses and support the validity of the organizational health construct.

A Comparison of Elements of School Health for Elementary, Middle, and High Schools

Given the fact that middle schools are different from elementary and secondary schools, it should not be surprising that a different

TABLE 3.6 Correlations Between Health Dimensions and Aspects of Trust ($N = 86$)

Measures of Organizational Health	Measures of Faculty Trust	
	Trust in Principal	Trust in Colleagues
Overall health	.64**	.36**
Technical level		
Academic Emphasis	.33**	.27*
Teacher Affiliation	.53**	.63**
Managerial level		
Collegial Leadership	.81**	.31**
Principal Influence	.27*	.06
Resource Support	.43**	.25*
Institutional level		
Institutional Integrity	.14	−.12

*$p < .05$; **$p < .01$.

measure of school health is useful for middle schools; in fact, there are three versions of the OHI, one for each level—elementary, middle, and high school. The conceptual foundations for all versions are the same, but the items and dimensions are slightly different depending on level. What are the basic differences?

Compared to high schools, both elementary and middle schools have more simple structures, a fact that is supported by the health profiles of each level of school. As one moves from elementary to middle to high school, the dimensions of health become increasingly differentiated as the structure becomes more complex. Teachers at all three school levels are concerned with institutional integrity, academic emphasis, and teacher morale or affiliation, but the leadership of the principal becomes more differentiated from elementary to middle to high school. At the elementary level, there are only two dimensions of leadership, collegial leadership and resource influence, but these two divide into four by high school. Resource influence divides into principal influence and resource support as one moves from the elementary to middle school, and collegial leadership behavior separates into initiating structure and consideration as one continues to the high school (see Table 3.8). As one might expect, the middle school is a hybrid of structure and complexity. The leadership of the

TABLE 3.7 Correlational and Multiple Regression Analyses: Correlations' Beta Weights Indicating Relative Importance of the Dimensions of School Health in Affecting Aspects of Faculty Trust ($N = 86$)

| Measures of Organizational Health | Measures of Faculty Trust | | | |
| | Trust in Principal | | Trust in Colleagues | |
	Correlation	Beta[a]	Correlation	Beta[a]
Technical Level				
Academic Emphasis	.33*	.01	.27*	.06
Teacher Affiliation	.53**	.17*	.63**	.66**
Managerial Level				
Collegial Leadership	.81**	.73**	.31**	.09
Principal Influence	.27*	.00	.06	−.09
Resource Support	.43**	.01	.25**	−.03
Institutional Level				
Institutional Integrity	.14	−.07	−.12	−.17
Multiple correlation (R)	.82**		.66**	

a. Beta weights are in standard measure.
*$p < .05$; **$p < .01$.

middle school principal is more integrated than high school principals but less integrated than elementary principals. The same can be said for the general complexity of health for middle schools.

Summary and Discussion

The OHI-M is a 45-item climate instrument with 6 dimensions that describe the behavior of middle school students, teachers, and principals. This instrument, unlike other versions of the OHI, was designed for use in middle schools. It measures two aspects of teacher and student behaviors—teacher affiliation and academic emphasis; three aspects of principal behavior—collegial leadership, resource support, and principal influence; and an institutional property called institutional integrity. Moreover, measures of these

TABLE 3.8 A Comparison of the Elements of School Health for Elementary, Middle, and High Schools

Elementary School	Middle School	High School
Institutional Integrity	Institutional Integrity	Institutional Integrity
Collegial Leadership	Collegial Leadership	Initiating Structure Consideration
Resource Influence	Resource Support Principal Influence	Resource Support Principal Influence
Teacher Affiliation	Teacher Affiliation	Morale
Academic Emphasis	Academic Emphasis	Academic Emphasis

six dimensions of teacher-student, teacher-teacher, and teacher-administrator relations can be combined to provide an overall index of general school health.

The properties of the measures of the six subtests of the OHI-M are strong. All the scales have high reliability coefficients. The factor structure is stable; it was similar for two separate samples. Furthermore, the empirical results of this study also provide strong construct-related evidence for the validity of dimensions of school health. In brief, the OHI-M is a stable, reliable, and valid measure of the organizational health of middle schools.

A healthy middle school is a pleasant place. It is protected from unwarranted intrusion (high institutional integrity). Teachers like the school, the students, and each other, and are enthusiastic about their work (high teacher affiliation). Teachers see students as serious and diligent in their learning (high academic emphasis). They see the principal as their ally in the improvement of instruction; the principal is friendly, open, respectful, and supportive, and yet establishes and is committed to high standards of teacher performance (strong collegial leadership). The principal also has influence with organizational superiors and is seen as someone who can deliver (high principal influence), as well as one who can get teachers the instructional materials they need (high resource support). The healthy school has no need to coerce cooperation; it is freely given by teacher professionals who are committed to teaching and learning.

The unhealthy middle school, by way of contrast, is a rather dismal place. Various pressure groups use the school as an arena to work out their own agendas (low institutional integrity). The principal is ineffective in moving the school toward its goals, and either out of frustration or inclination, attempts to move teachers with a heavy hand (weak collegial leadership). The principal has little influence with superiors (low principal influence) and teachers are unable to get the instructional materials and supplies that they request (weak resource support). Teachers are not committed to their work; they don't like the kids, the school, or their colleagues (weak teacher affiliation). Moreover, teachers view students as uncooperative; students do not work hard, do not do their homework, and are not serious about learning (low academic emphasis). No one is especially happy in the unhealthy school; it cries out for leadership and change.

As we expected, school health is positively related to faculty trust in both the principal and in colleagues. In general, trust complements healthy interpersonal interactions. But the relationship between health and trust is a little more complicated than it seems at first blush. Consistent with earlier findings in elementary and high schools (Tarter, Bliss, & Hoy, 1989; Tarter & Hoy, 1988), different dimensions of organizational health are associated with different aspects of faculty trust. The leadership of the principal is strongly related to faculty trust in the principal. Not surprisingly, the collegial leadership of the principal is most important in generating faculty trust in the principal; specifically, leadership that is open, supportive, and friendly, and that treats teachers as equals is strongly related to trust in the principal. Teacher affiliation makes only a minor secondary contribution to faculty trust in the principal. In contrast, teacher affiliation is strongly related to faculty trust in colleagues, whereas none of the dimensions of principal leadership make a unique, significant contribution to faculty trust in colleagues. The teacher group, not the principal, is critical in developing an atmosphere of trust among colleagues. When teachers like their students, their school, and each other, they are more likely to trust one another, and conversely, when they trust each other, they are more likely to be positive about students, school, and colleagues. The finding that principal behavior is associated with trust in the principal and teacher behavior with trust in colleagues, although not surprising, is provocative. Clearly, there are limits to what a principal can do in generating a culture of trust.

Implications

The construct of school health, like openness in school climate, has theoretical, research, and practical implications. Regardless of one's focus, the development of the OHI-M opens up a host of opportunities.

Theory and Research

A healthy organizational climate should be a goal in itself. Not only is organizational health a worthy end that is indispensable to purposive organizational dynamics, but it is likely a means to quality schools. Schools should be places where teachers and students want to be rather than have to be. Healthy schools are such places; they are places were students feel good about themselves and their teachers; teachers respect their students and have confidence in their ability to succeed. Trust among and between teachers and administrators is high in healthy schools.

A key to successful leadership is to influence organization members (Bennis, 1989; Hoy et al., 1991; Pelz, 1952). In middle schools, the collegial principal will likely foster participation and cooperation among teachers. Leadership that is collegial encourages teacher initiation, is supportive, and is stimulating without being threatening. Collegial relations between teachers and principals seem indispensable if schools are to become truly professional organizations. Hoy and Forsyth (1986) and Sergiovanni (1991, 1992) maintain that effective supervision is only possible when relationships between supervisors and teachers are open, collegial, and nonthreatening. As with the openness of school climate, school health seems crucial for effective and productive long-term relationships.

The OHI-M is a heuristic research tool. The construct suggests a host of important research questions. For example, to what extent does school health affect such student outcomes as self-concept, commitment to school, motivation, absenteeism, and vandalism? To what extent does school health facilitate quality middle schools? Is school health related to faculty trust in students? To student trust in teachers? To student achievement?

Research is emerging that links certain aspects of school health with student achievement in mathematics, reading, and writing (Hannum, 1994; Hoy & Hannum, 1997; see Chapter 4, this volume). What are the antecedents to healthy middle schools? How do schools become healthy places to work and study? To what extent and how do structural changes in middle schools affect the school health?

The concept of school health developed in this research is a framework for the study of a myriad of processes as well as outcomes in school organizations. For example, to what extent is school health related to such organizational processes as leadership, motivation, communication, decision making, goal setting, discipline, and control?

Collegial leadership is integrated; it combines a need to get the task done with the need for individuals to fulfill their needs. When and how can principals move to a more collegial style? No one leadership style, not even a collegial one, is successful in all situations. What are the necessary conditions for successful collegial leadership? How do principals develop a climate of openness and trust that is conducive to autonomous and professional teacher leadership? The list of research possibilities goes on.

Practice

The health perspective reveals a number of more immediate and practical issues. Administrators can use the notion of organizational health and well-being as a way to organize, analyze, assess, and guide behavior in schools. Principals often informally classify what happens in a school in terms of how well they are doing or how teachers react. The health framework provides another perspective for middle school principals to reflect about how they are doing. How healthy are the interpersonal dynamics of their school? How well do teachers like their school, their students, and each other? How committed are teachers to helping students achieve? Do teachers feel they have the necessary instructional materials and supplies to do the job? How supportive and collegial is the principal's leadership? Does the principal use his or her influence to go to bat for teachers? In short, the school health framework is another organizational and conceptual guide for administrator self-reflection and analysis.

The OHI-M, like the OCDQ-RM, can be used in a more formal way. It is easy to administer to faculty, easy to score, and easy to interpret; in fact, using the norms developed in the current study, it is possible to determine the well-being and health of school climate.[1] Teachers do not mind; in fact, they rather enjoy responding to the instrument. A mere 10 minutes of a faculty meeting and it's done. The instrument not only identifies those schools that are or are not healthy, but it pinpoints those aspects of the school health that are undesirable and in need of amelioration. For example, poor health may be a function of teachers' perceptions of the principal's leadership behavior. Teachers may describe the principal as one who has no influence, cannot get the needed resources, and does not express clear expectations. The principal may be surprised by such perceptions and protest that the teachers are wrong or inaccurate. As we have already suggested, it really doesn't matter who is right or wrong; the principal has a problem if the teachers have a perception of a nonsupportive and uninfluential manager. The principal needs to determine the source of the discrepancies. One intriguing outcome of the analysis of school health is uncovering inconsistencies in perceptions between the principal and the faculty (see Chapter 5). Formal analyses of organizational health are useful from time to time because they provide a more systematic way to evaluate the teacher-teacher and teacher-principal relations than personal impressions.

Finally, like the OCDQ-RM, the OHI-M can be used for inservice and professional development. Administrations of these instruments can gauge the success of the improvement interventions, identify areas in need of change, and produce a basis for dialogue and cooperation among teachers and administrators. Some superintendents might be tempted to use these instruments for school evaluation. We repeat. Don't. Such summative assessments will undermine the utility of the measures for self-improvement and organizational development.

We also remind you that profiles of school health and openness are snapshots of the school. The pictures do not explain why things are the way they are; they merely describe perceptions, albeit important ones. Those who find their schools in need of change must discover the causes of the existing conditions before they can adequately improve the workplace. Those concerned with the health of middle schools now have an easy, inexpensive, and accurate tool with which to guide their efforts.

In this chapter and the previous one, we have presented the conceptual and empirical bases for viewing and measuring two complementary frameworks of organizational climate—openness and health. Before we provide examples for using the frameworks to evaluate and improve the environment of schools, we examine and explore the relationships between organizational climate and quality schools in the next chapter.

Note

1. Scores are standardized with a mean of 500 and a standard deviation of 100 and are interpreted the same as SAT or GRE scores. See Chapter 5 for details.

CHAPTER

4

RESEARCH FINDINGS ON SCHOOL OPENNESS, SCHOOL HEALTH, AND SCHOOL QUALITY

In general, the clarification of concepts . . . is a frequent result of empirical research. Research sensitive to its own needs cannot easily escape this pressure of conceptual clarification. For a basic requirement of research is the concepts, variables, be defined with sufficient clarity to enable the research to proceed.

Robert K. Merton, 1957,
Social Theory and Social Structure

The two instruments developed in this book, the OCDQ-RM and the OHI-M, are relatively new, yet a substantial body of empirical research supports the significance of climate as an integral part of successful schools. In this chapter we examine the extent to which health and openness of school climate are indicators of quality schools. In particular, we use the framework of quality indicators

79

outlined in the first chapter and test their empirical interrelationships with climate. Finally, the chapter concludes with some observations and implications for practitioners and researchers.

A Methodological Note

Before proceeding with the research findings of our study, we
describe the sample of schools and the procedures that were used to
collect the data. All of the findings in this chapter came from the
same large and diverse sample of middle schools. All the variables
that are examined are indicators of quality schools. As each element
of the research unfolds, the new concepts and measures will be explained.

Sample

The unit of analysis for climate studies should be the school because the variables reflect organizational properties (Hoy, Tarter, &
Kottkamp, 1991; Sirotnik, 1980). A sample of 87 middle schools,
which included responses from 2,777 teachers, was used to refine
and confirm the structure of the instrument and then to test several
hypotheses about climate and authenticity.

The sample of middle schools was drawn from New Jersey. Although it was not possible to select a random sample of New Jersey
middle schools, care was taken to select urban, suburban, and rural
schools from diverse geographic areas of the state as well as from all
socioeconomic levels in the state. Only schools that called themselves
middle schools and had a 5-8, 6-8, or 7-8 configuration were included
in the sample. Extremely small middle schools were not part of the
sample; schools with fewer than 15 faculty members were not considered for the sample. Using the state's measure of socioeconomic
status, 28% of the schools came from the lowest levels, 38% came
from the middle levels, and 34% came from the highest levels. Fifteen
of the 21 counties in New Jersey were represented in the sample.[1]

Socioeconomic Status

The socioeconomic status (SES) of a school was measured by use
of the state district factor groups (DFG). DFG is a composite index of
SES based on a factor composed of the following variables: educa-

tional level of adults in the district, the occupations of adults in the district, the percentage of people who have lived in the district for the past 10 years, the number of people per housing unit, the percentage of urban population in the district, average family income, and rate of unemployment and poverty. Districts are arrayed along a continuum of 1 to 10; the higher the number, the greater the SES. Thus, the DFG computed by the state of New Jersey is our measure of SES.

Data Collection

Data were collected from all teachers at regularly scheduled faculty meetings. The purpose of the study was explained in general terms, anonymity was guaranteed, and the importance of candid responses was emphasized. Teachers at the meeting were divided into three random groups with one group responding to the OHI-M, another to the OCDQ-RM, and the third to other measures of school properties such as faculty participation, trust, perceptions of effectiveness, and culture. This procedure was used because the unit of analysis was the school (data were aggregated at the school level), because it ensured methodological separation of the variables, and because it was an efficient method for collecting a large amount of data without overburdening teachers. Virtually everyone in attendance responded to one of the instruments. Data were collected by members of the research team (Kevin Barnes, John Hannum, James Hoffman, and Dennis Sabo) over a 3-month period.

School Climate and Student Achievement

Some empirical evidence links school climate and achievement (Armor et al., 1976; Bossert, 1988; Brookover et al., 1979). In many studies, after a small number of "effective" and "ineffective" schools are identified, researchers then catalog organizational characteristics attempting to find consistent differences between the two types of schools. Not surprisingly, the differences vary from study to study when such post hoc methods are used, and the list of effective school attributes grows as more such studies are done. In the general literature, school climate is typically a global construct that researchers use loosely to group together studies of school environment, learning environment, learning climate, sense of community, leadership, academic climate, and social climate. Therein lies both the strength and the weakness of the climate construct; it is a useful integrating concept on one hand, but on the other, it suffers from a lack of clear definition. In this book, we consistently use the terms openness and health to refer to school climate. Thus, a guiding question of this study is, "To what extent are aspects of the openness and health of climate related to student achievement and other school quality indicators?"

Another important issue emerges in our analyses. Does school climate improve student achievement or does high student achievement produce a better school climate? We posit an interdependent and reciprocal relationship (Homans, 1950). School climate affects student achievement, but the reverse is also true: Student achievement affects school climate. The two are mutually dependent.

A caveat is also in order. We do not equate high student achievement with school effectiveness. Although achievement is one aspect of school effectiveness, it is not the whole of it. School effectiveness is much more complex and includes many other outcomes such as social-emotional growth of students, satisfaction of teachers, efficient use of resources, innovativeness, adaptability, and goal accomplishment (Cameron & Whetton, 1983, 1995; Hoy & Miskel, 1991, 1996). As we explained in Chapter 1, in assessing schools, we prefer the notion of quality over effectiveness because quality encompasses means as well as ends. We explore the quality of both important means such as climate openness and health as well as ends such as achievement and trust.

Student achievement is clearly a critical end product of schooling. The focus of our analysis of achievement is on basic skills—reading, writing, and arithmetic. Higher-order thinking and problem-solving skills are also important student outcomes, but they are not considered in this research because of their lack of consistent measures among school districts we studied. On the other hand, data using the same measures of basic achievement were available for all schools in our sample because they were collected by the state in the eighth grade at the conclusion of the middle school experience.

Student Achievement

Student achievement was measured using the state of New Jersey's Eighth-Grade Early Warning Test (EWT), which is given to all eighth-grade students in the state. The test measures achievement in reading, mathematics, and writing using both multiple-choice and constructed-response items. The reading section of the examination had a reliability of .84, the mathematics section a reliability of .89, and the writing task a reliability of .92. All achievement data were obtained by the researchers directly from the New Jersey State Department of Education.

Climate Measures

The instruments to measure the openness and health of school climate have been described in detail in Chapters 2 and 3 and will not be repeated here except to note that both the OCDQ-RM and the OHI-M are reliable and valid measures of school climate.

Empirical Findings

The relationships between climate and achievement will be examined from several vantage points. We begin our analyses with the general notions of health and openness and proceed to the more specific aspects of each construct.

Openness, Health, and Achievement. In the last two chapters, three general indexes of school climate were offered—school health, openness of the principal's behavior, and openness of the teachers' behavior. We began by simply looking at the correlations among these aspects of climate and three measures of student achievement in reading, writing, and mathematics. Given the general literature on school climate and student achievement (Armor et al., 1976; Bossert, 1988; Brookover et al., 1979), we expected positive relationships. As predicted, health and openness were related to all three measures of student achievement. Health of the school climate had significant relationships with the measures of student achievement ($r = .61, .58,$ and .55 for math, reading, and writing, respectively). The same is true of the openness of the principal's behavior ($r = .52, .54,$ and .47 for math, reading, and writing, respectively) and the openness of teachers' behavior ($r = .42, .40,$ and .42 for math, reading, and writing, respectively). Not surprisingly, the health and openness measures were also significantly correlated with each other. All of the correlations are summarized in Table 4.1.

TABLE 4.1 Correlations Among General Aspects of School
Climate and Measures of Student Achievement

Variable	Principal Openness	Teacher Openness	School Health	Math	Reading	Writing
Principal openness	1.00	.50**	.70**	.52**	.54**	.47**
Teacher openness		1.00	.57**	.42**	.40**	.42**
School health			1.00	.61**	.58**	.55**
Math				1.00	.97**	.89**
Reading					1.00	.92**
Writing						1.00

**$p < .01$

Dimensions of Openness and Student Achievement. Next we examined how all the dimensions of the OCDQ-RM, both collectively and individually, explain the variance in student achievement. Multiple regression analysis is well-suited in this regard because it enables the researcher to determine not only the effect of one variable independent of the others, but also the combined effect of the independent variables (climate) on the dependent (achievement).

The OCDQ-RM has six dimensions: Supportive, Directive, and Restrictive behaviors, which describe the principal's leader behavior; and Collegial, Committed, and Disengaged, which depict teacher behaviors. Firestone and Wilson (1985) found that principal support was positively related to student outcomes, whereas close and rigid control was negatively associated with these outcomes; other researchers and theorists (Corwin & Borman, 1988; Rosenholtz, 1985) have suggested similar relationships. Likewise, there is widespread agreement that teacher collegiality and teacher commitment are important forces in improving teacher practice and getting better results (Barth, 1990; Rosenholtz, 1989; Sergiovanni, 1992). Thus, our prediction was straightforward: *Factors that promote openness in both teacher-teacher and teacher-principal relationships also promote higher levels of student achievement in reading, writing, and mathematics.*

This general hypothesis was tested several ways. First, each aspect of climate was correlated with each element of achievement with the expectation that supportive principal behavior and collegial and committed teacher behavior would be positively related to achievement; and, directive and restrictive principal behavior and disengaged teacher behavior would be negatively related to achievement. Then, for a finer picture of the relationship, each aspect of student achievement was regressed on all six dimensions of the openness of organizational climate. Finally, because what often seems to be a strong predictor of achievement is often a proxy for socioeconomic level (SES), we did a second set of regressions in which SES is included as a predictor variable along with the climate dimensions. Thus, we control for the impact of SES, and at the same time, determine the independent influence of SES and each climate variable as well as their combined effect.

The correlation analysis strongly supported the openness-achievement hypothesis. With the exception of disengagement, each of the elements of climate openness had significant and strong-to-moderate correlations with all aspects of student achievement. Disengagement was significantly related to only writing achievement. A lack of restrictiveness in the leadership of the principal as well as collegial and committed teachers seem to be the elements of openness that most strongly are related to achievement. See Table 4.2 for a summary of the correlations.

In general, the regression analyses supported that same picture. A lack of principal restrictiveness coupled with collegial and committed teacher behavior are the best predictors of achievement (see Table 4.3). Panel A of Table 4.3 shows that the six climate dimensions have multiple Rs of .69, .68, and .61 with math, reading, and writing achievement scores and explain 44%, 42%, and 33% of the variance for the respective tests. Disengagement makes virtually no independent contribution to the explanation of achievement variance. When SES is added as a variable in the regression equations, only collegial teacher behavior and a lack of restrictive principal behavior make significant independent contributions to the mathematics achievement variance. Similar patterns appear for reading and writing, but they are not as strong. Not surprisingly, SES is the single most important predictor of high student achievement. Panel B of Table 4.3 shows that the six climate dimensions combined with SES have multiple Rs of .83, .81, and .75 with math, reading, and writing achievement scores and explain 66%, 62%, and 52% of the variance for the respective tests.

TABLE 4.2 Correlations of Elements of Openness and Aspects of
Student Achievement ($N = 87$)

Elements of Openness in Organizational Climate	Measures of Student Achievement		
	Math	Reading	Writing
Supportive	.28**	.32**	.30**
Directive	−.37**	−.37**	−.31**
Restrictive	−.60**	−.61**	−.52**
Collegial	.43**	.40**	.42**
Committed	.40**	.37**	.38**
Disengaged	−.14	−.17	−.19*

*$p < .05$; **$p < .01$ (one-tailed tests).

Dimensions of Health and Student Achievement. We now consider
the extent to which the dimensions of the OHI-M, both collectively
and individually, explain the variance in student achievement. As
with our analysis of the dimensions of openness, we begin with
simple correlational analysis and progress to multiple regression.

The OHI-M has six dimensions: Academic Emphasis and
Teacher Affiliation describe the teachers' behavior; Collegial Leadership, Resource Support, and Principal Influence depict principal behavior; and Institutional Integrity portrays the relationship between
the school and the community. Earlier research at the secondary level
showed the significance of academic emphasis in fostering student
achievement (Bryk, Lee, & Holland, 1993; Hoy et al., 1991; Murphy,
Weil, Hallinger, & Mitman, 1982; Shouse & Brinson, 1995). Teacher
affiliation also captures many of the features of teacher-teacher interactions (e.g., strong affiliation with colleagues and with the school,
commitment to students, and cooperation) that have been associated
with student achievement.

Principals can influence teaching either by administrative support or administrative control. Support clearly seems more effective
than control (Corwin & Borman, 1988). Principal support includes
respecting and treating teachers as colleagues as well as using influence with superiors to help teachers get the resources they need.

Previous research in high schools has unexpectedly revealed a
negative relationship between Institutional Integrity and student
achievement. When teachers perceive "interference" in the school
from the community, students achieve at higher levels. Clearly,

TABLE 4.3 Multiple Regression Analysis of Elements of Openness With Aspects of Student Achievement ($N = 87$)

Measures of Elements of Climate Openness	Panel A			Panel B		
	Student Achievement Standard Beta Weights			Regression Includes SES Student Achievement Standard Beta Weights		
	Math	Read	Write	Math	Read	Write
Supportive	−.18	−.11	−.08	−.11	−.05	−.02
Directive	−.11	−.08	−.02	−.10	−.07	.01
Restrictive	−.52**	−.54**	−.44**	−.24**	−.27**	−.18†
Collegial	.23*	.18	.23*	.17*	.13	.17
Committed	.21**	.16	.16	.11	.06	.07
Disengaged	.05	.00	−.03	.08	.03	.00
SES				.56**	.54**	.53**
R	.69**	.68**	.61**	.83**	.81**	.75**
Adjusted R^2	.44	.42	.33	.66	.62	.52

$*p < .05;$ $**p < .01;$ † = .06.

teachers do not like such interference, but negative effects on student achievement are not the case; in fact, just the opposite seems true.

In sum, the literature and theory suggest that collegial principals who are friendly, open, egalitarian, and committed to excellence are most likely to create a school climate conducive to student achievement. Likewise, teachers who are committed to students, their colleagues, and their school, who set high but achievable academic goals for students, and who are cohesive and cooperative rather than critical and divisive, are likely to produce a climate conducive to student learning. Finally, if schools have healthy internal interpersonal relations among students, teachers, and the principal, and simultaneously, interested parents pressure school authorities to initiate new programs and are critical of existing ones, then student achievement is positively influenced. Thus, our general hypothesis is as follows: *Except for Institutional Integrity, factors that facilitate healthy interpersonal relations among principals, teachers, and students promote higher levels of student achievement in reading, writing, and mathematics.*[2]

The correlation analysis strongly supported the health-achievement hypothesis. With the exception of principal influence, all the elements of school health had significant and strong-to-moderate bivariate correlations with all the aspects of student achievement. As expected, and consistent with other research, Institutional Integrity was significantly and negatively related to student achievement. Academic Emphasis, Teacher Affiliation, and Resource Support were the elements of organizational health that had substantial bivariate correlations with achievement in math, reading, and writing. See Table 4.4 for a summary of the correlations.

The regression analyses support and refine the picture portrayed by the correlational analyses. Academic Emphasis, Teacher Affiliation, Resource Support, and a negative Institutional Integrity are the key elements of health that foster high student achievement in basic skills (see Table 4.5). Panel A of Table 4.5 shows that the six health elements have multiple Rs of .84, .82, and .77 with math, reading, and writing achievement scores and explain 68%, 64%, and 56% of the variance for the respective tests. Principal Influence and Collegial Leadership make virtually no independent contribution to the explanation of achievement variance. When SES is added as a variable in the regression equation, the pattern of relationships remains quite similar. Although SES is the single most important predictor of high student achievement, four other health elements provide substantial and significant independent effects on various aspects of student achievement. Panel B of Table 4.5 shows that the six health elements of organizational climate combined with SES have multiple Rs of .88, .86, and .81 with math, reading, and writing achievement scores and explain 75%, 71%, and 62% of the variance for the respective tests.

Conclusion

The results of our analyses have demonstrated a significant and positive relationship between school climate and student achievement. In general, the more open and healthy the school climate, the greater the levels of student achievement in the basic skills of reading, writing, and mathematics. Some aspects of openness and health are more important than others. For example, nonrestrictiveness of the principal and collegial teacher relations seem especially important elements of openness, and Academic Emphasis, Teacher Affiliation, and Resource Support are central elements of health that foster student achievement. Although teachers like to be buffered from outside forces, schools that feel pressure from the community are

TABLE 4.4 Correlations of Elements of Health and Aspects of
Student Achievement (*N* = 86)

Elements of Health in Organizational Climate	Math	Reading	Writing
	Measures of Student Achievement		
Academic Emphasis	.73**	.70**	.64**
Teacher Affiliation	.53**	.51**	.51**
Collegial Leadership	.28**	.28**	.25*
Resource Support	.50**	.50**	.46**
Principal Influence	.17	.13	.15
Institutional Integrity	−.36**	−.36**	−.35**

*p < .05; **p < .01 (one-tailed tests).

more likely to have higher levels of student achievement. The relationship between Institutional Integrity and student achievement is neither simple nor clear, and it is a topic to which we will return later in this chapter. Finally, it is encouraging to find that some aspects of school climate are related to student achievement regardless of the SES of the community. Although not easy to effect, school climate is more amenable to change than the SES of a school (see Chapter 5).

School Climate and Overall School Effectiveness

Student achievement is simply one aspect of quality schools albeit an important one. We now examine some other indicators of quality that combine to represent overall school effectiveness. The measures of school effectiveness that we explore are perceptual; that is, they represent the perceptions of teachers about how effective their schools are—they are subjective assessments.

Overall School Effectiveness

Paul Mott (1972) has formulated and tested a model of organizational effectiveness that has a number of critical elements:

- Quantity and quality of the product
- Efficiency

TABLE 4.5 Multiple Regression Analysis of Elements of Health and Climate With Aspects of Student Achievement (N = 86)

Measures of Elements of Health in Organizational Climate	Panel A Student Achievement Standard Beta Weights			Panel B Regression Includes SES Student Achievement Standard Beta Weights		
	Math	Read	Write	Math	Read	Write
Academic Emphasis	.49**	.44**	.37**	.28**	.22*	.16
Teacher Affiliation	.24**	.21**	.27**	.20**	.17*	.23*
Collegial Leadership	.04	.07	.02	.04	.07	.03
Resource Support	.15	.20*	.18*	.14	.19*	.17
Principal Influence	−.02	−.06	−.02	−.04	−.08	−.04
Institutional Integrity	−.38**	−.39**	−.38**	−.28**	−.29**	−.29**
SES				.36**	.38**	.35**
Multiple R	.84**	.82**	.77**	.88**	.86**	.81**
Adjusted R²	.68	.64	.56	.75	.71	.62

*p < .05; **p < .01 (one-tailed tests).

- Adaptability
- Flexibility

Mott theorizes that these key elements of the organization define the ability of an organization to mobilize its centers of power for action to achieve goals and to adapt to external and internal constraints. Effective organizations are efficient in achieving quality outcomes and successful in coping with internal and external strains. The model seems appropriate for examining the effectiveness of different kinds of organizations including public schools.

Mott (1972) tested his formulation in the study of a variety of organizations. First, he developed an eight-item index of effectiveness based on his model, and then validated this perceptual measure of general effectiveness by demonstrating its consistent, positive relationships with other objective measures of effectiveness in several different kinds of organizations. Mott concluded that the evidence from his research suggested, with appropriate safeguards, that subjective evaluations of employees provided a fairly valid measure of organizational effectiveness. Miskel and his colleagues (Miskel, DeFrain, & Wilcox, 1980; Miskel, Fevurly, & Stewart, 1979) were the first educational researchers to adapt and use Mott's theory and measure to study the organizational effectiveness of schools. Hoy and Ferguson (1985) later provided empirical evidence to support both the validity and reliability of the measure of effectiveness for public schools.

An Index of Perceived Organizational Effectiveness

The measure of effectiveness used here is derived from Mott's work as adapted by Miskel and his colleagues. A complete copy of the index is found in Hoy and Miskel (1991, 1996). A few examples give the flavor of the index:

- How good is the quality of the products and services produced by people you know in your school? (Quality)
- How efficiently do people in your school do their work? (Efficiency)
- How good a job is done by the people in your school in anticipating problems and preventing them from occurring or minimizing their effects? (Adaptability)
- How good a job do the people in your school do in coping with emergencies and disruptions? (Flexibility)

Because the measure of Mott's concept of organizational effectiveness was based on a number of different elements, we decided to check the dimensionality of the index by factoring the eight items. The results supported one strong dimension of overall effectiveness: all the items loaded strongly on the first factor (the loadings ranged from .72 to .91) and explained 68% of the variance. An alpha coefficient of reliability for the effectiveness index in the current sample of schools was .93, a value that is consistent with earlier research (Hoy & Ferguson, 1985).

Empirical Findings

If the index is a reasonable gauge of overall effectiveness, then it should be highly correlated with such other quality measures of schools as openness, health, and student achievement. To that end, we correlated our measures of openness, health, and student achievement with the index of effectiveness. As predicted, all of our measures of quality were substantially and significantly correlated with the index of effectiveness (the range of r was .50 to .67). The results clearly support the concurrent validity of the index as an overall measure of effectiveness and quality. Overall effectiveness was not only positively correlated with principal openness ($r = .52$, $p < .01$), teacher openness ($r = .50, p < .01$), and health ($r = .67, p < .01$) but was strongly related to student achievement in math ($r = .61$, $p < .01$), reading ($r = .60, p < .01$), and writing ($r = .58, p < .01$). The openness and health variables also combine to explain 41% of the variance of effectiveness ($R = .64, p < .01$).

Conclusion

Again we find that the openness and health of school climate are strongly related to quality schools. Open and healthy school climate is positively and significantly correlated with overall school effectiveness; such schools are judged by teachers to have better products and services, to be more efficient, and to be more flexible and adaptable.

School Climate and Measures of Culture

We use the concept of culture to identify another set of quality indicators of schools. Organizational culture is a system of orientations (norms, core values, and tacit assumptions) shared by members, which hold the unit together and give it a distinctive identity. Because it is difficult to assess the culture of the school directly, we map the culture indirectly, first by conceptualizing critical dimensions of school culture, and then by developing a set of scales to measure each element.

Elements of Strong School Cultures

If there is one thing that students of organization agree on it is that culture refers to a set of shared perspectives that gives the organization a distinctive character (Anderson, 1982; Denison, 1996; Miskel & Ogawa, 1988; Ouchi & Wilkins, 1985). We have identified five elements that seem to characterize strong school cultures:

- Shared identity
- Trust
- Authenticity
- Cooperation
- Participation

We posited that if schools are to be successful they must develop a strong shared identity, one that embraces the values of trust, authenticity, cooperation, and shared participation. Now we turn to the empirical test of this proposition.

Climate and Shared Identity

Shared identity refers to the extent to which an organization has a clear vision, a distinctive mission, a set of shared means to achieve its goals, and participants who believe that their organization stands for something different and special.[3] The concept was operationalized by a scale consisting of the following eight Likert-type items:

- My school stands for something distinctive in society.
- My school has definite ideas about how things should be done.
- My school has a distinctive mission.
- My school has a clear view about how to achieve goals.
- My school has a clear vision of its role in society.
- My school produces a special kind of student.
- My school produces a special kind of teacher.
- My school's trademark is a special style of management.

The unidimensionality of the scale was supported by a principal components factor analysis that identified only one factor, which explained 72% of the variance. An alpha coefficient for the shared identity scale was .94.

Empirical Findings. If shared identity is a characteristic of quality schools, then it should be significantly related to other quality measures of schools; consequently, we correlated our measures of effectiveness, openness, health, and student achievement with the shared identity scale. An examination of the correlations in Table 4.6 reveals that, as predicted, all of our measures of quality significantly correlated with shared identity (the range of r was .29 to .69). The correlations are summarized in Table 4.6

Climate and Trust

Trust is a critical element of effective interpersonal relationships in schools (Hoffman, Sabo, Bliss, & Hoy, 1994); it is critical to effective leadership (Bennis, 1989); and in fact, Sergiovanni (1991) has claimed that it is indispensable to moral leadership. We have defined trust as general confidence and overall optimism in occurring events—believing in others in the absence of compelling reasons to disbelieve. In the context of organizations, trust is a work group's generalized expectancy that the words, actions, and promises of another individual or group can be relied on (Hoy & Kupersmith, 1985). Individuals trust others not only to be consistent in action but to act with good intentions.

In the current analysis, we examined faculty trust as it was expressed toward the principal and fellow teachers. In particular, two aspects of faculty trust were the foci:

- *Trust in the Principal.* The faculty has confidence that the principal will keep his or her word and act in the best interest of teachers.
- *Trust in Colleagues.* The faculty believes that teachers can depend on each other in difficult situations and that teachers can rely on the integrity of their colleagues.

TABLE 4.6 Correlations Among Measures of School Quality

Variable	Overall Effectiveness	Principal Openness	Teacher Openness	School Health	Math	Reading	Writing
Overall effectiveness	1.00	.52**	.50**	.67**	.61**	.60**	.58**
Shared identity	.69**	.50**	.45**	.64**	.32**	.29**	.31**
Trust in principal	.56**	.68**	.47**	.65**	.30**	.30**	.27**
Trust in colleagues	.72**	.35**	.55**	.42**	.40**	.39**	.38**
Leader authenticity	.46**	.72**	.37**	.72**	.36**	.37**	.29**
Teacher authenticity	.43**	.38**	.57**	.65**	.30**	.27**	.24*
Teacher cooperation	.57**	.45**	.73**	.61**	.37**	.36**	.36**
Participation	.66**	.56**	.41**	.65**	.58**	.58**	.58**

$*p < .05$; $**p < .01$ (one-tailed tests).

These two aspects of trust were measured by the Faculty Trust Scales developed by Hoy and Kupersmith (1985). The dimensions of the scales were confirmed in the current sample through factor-analytic techniques (see Hoffman et al., 1994). Teachers were asked to describe their interpersonal relations and feelings along a 6-point Likert-type scale from *strongly disagree* to *strongly agree*. Two sample items for each scale are as follows:

Trust in the Principal
  • Teachers in this school trust the principal.
  • Teachers often question the motives of the principal (score reversed).

Trust in Colleagues
  • Teachers in this school typically look out for each other.
  • Teachers take unfair advantage of each other in this school (score reversed).

The two trust measures were each composed of seven items. Both scales are highly reliable with alpha coefficients of reliability in the current study at .86 for faculty trust in the principal and .91 for faculty trust in colleagues. The evidence suggesting construct validity of the scales is supported by two factor-analytic studies (Hoffman et al., 1994; Hoy & Kupersmith, 1985).

Empirical Findings. Like the other elements of culture, we expected both aspects of trust to be significantly related to other quality measures of schools. Our expectations were confirmed. When we correlated our measures of effectiveness, openness, health, and student achievement with the trust measures, we found that trust was significantly associated with all of the other quality indicators (the range of r was .27 to .72). The correlations are summarized in Table 4.6.

Climate and Authenticity

Authenticity is yet another important aspect of productive school cultures. We assume that long-term productivity cannot occur in an atmosphere of game playing, trickery, and phoniness. A culture of charades and masquerades inhibits quality. At one level, it is quite easy to advocate authenticity, but it is quite a different matter to define the concept so that it can be operationalized and assessed.

Although there have been numerous attempts (Brumbaugh, 1971; Halpin, 1966; Henderson & Hoy, 1982; Seeman, 1966) to define the term, the results have produced mixed success. For purposes of this inquiry, however, the framework developed by Henderson and Hoy (1982) is useful (see Chapter 2, this volume). Authentic behavior consists of three basic aspects:

- Accountability—a willingness of organizational participants to accept responsibility, personal as well as organizational, for mistakes as well as negative outcomes.
- Nonmanipulation—colleagues or subordinates are not used for one's own purposes.
- Salience of self over role—role is subordinated to self; basic personality is a prime motivator of behavior, not some prescribed role.

In sum, authentic behavior is characterized by a willingness to accept responsibility for behavior, especially when the results are not positive; behavior that is nonmanipulative of others; and behavior in which role is subordinated to self.

Two measures of authenticity were used to tap genuine behavior in schools—perceptions of authentic teacher and principal behaviors. The authenticity scales were drawn from the work of Hoy and his colleagues (Henderson & Hoy, 1982; Hoy & Henderson, 1983; Hoy, Hoffman, Sabo, & Bliss, 1996). Items were constructed to capture the aspects of authenticity proposed by Henderson and Hoy— accountability, nonmanipulation, and salience of self over role. Examples of items include the following:

Principal Authenticity
- The principal is willing to admit mistakes when they are made.
- The principal manipulates teachers (score reversed).

Teacher Authenticity
- The teachers' beliefs and actions are consistent.
- Teachers here accept and learn from mistakes.

The authenticity scales were each composed of 16 Likert-type items. Both scales are reliable with alpha coefficients of reliability in the current study at .92 for principal authenticity and .88 for teacher authenticity. The evidence suggesting construct validity of the scales is supported by a number of factor-analytic studies (Henderson & Hoy, 1982; Hoffman, 1993; Hoy, Hoffman, et al., 1996). Factor analysis of the 32 items designed to measure teacher and principal authenticity supported the two separate aspects of authenticity.

Empirical Findings. We hypothesized that both of our measures of school authenticity would be significantly correlated with quality measures of schools, and they were. All measures of effectiveness, openness, health, and student achievement with the trust measures correlated significantly with both indexes of authenticity (the range of r was .24 to .72). The correlations are summarized in Table 4.6.

Climate and Cooperation

Cooperation is yet another aspect of strong cultures and productive organizations. Indeed, Ouchi's early analysis (1981) of American and Japanese organizations underscored the importance of cooperation as a core value of the cultures of effective organizations. In the present study, cooperation refers to schools in which teachers like each other, help each other, don't take advantage of each other, and support one another. Cooperation is the sense of teamwork and "pulling together" among teachers that imbues the school.

To measure this conception of cooperation, we asked teachers in each school to consider the extent to which eight behaviors characterized their schools. Then we created an index of school cooperation comprised of the following eight Likert-type items:

- Teachers in this school typically look out for each other.
- Teachers help and support each other.
- Teachers in this school like each other.
- Teachers exhibit friendliness to each other.
- Teachers volunteer to help each other.
- Teachers do favors for each other.

- Teachers here manipulate each other (score reversed).
- Teachers provide strong social support for colleagues.

The cooperation index had an alpha coefficient of .91, and a principal components factor analysis demonstrated the unidimensionality of the scale by identifying only one strong factor, which accounted for 66% of the variance.

Empirical Findings. As with the other elements of culture, we anticipated that cooperation would be significantly correlated with the our measures of school quality, and they were. Overall effectiveness, openness, health, and student achievement correlated significantly and substantially with our index of teacher cooperation in schools (the range of r was .36 to .73). The correlations are summarized in Table 4.6.

Climate and Participation

Participation is the final element of culture that we examined in our empirical analyses. Participation is the extent to which the teachers of a school believe that they are involved in the critical instructional decisions of a school; that is, they are involved with administrators and colleagues in making important professional judgments in such areas as teaching, developing learning goals, selecting textbooks and instructional materials, and developing student assessment procedures. Sixteen such critical areas formed the basis for determining the degree of participation. Participation was not measured in absolute terms but rather as the degree to which teachers wanted to and were involved in crucial professional decisions. Teachers in each school were asked two questions: how much they desired to be involved in decision making in each area and how much they were actually involved. Our index of participation was the difference between their desired and actual participation. Most researchers (Alutto & Belasco, 1972; Bacharach, Bauer, & Conely, 1986; Conway, 1976) describe the difference between desired and actual participation in terms of decision deprivation. In our analyses, a high level of participation refers to a low degree of deprivation. That is, a school had high participation to the extent that teachers were involved in the decisions in which they desired to be involved.

A set of critical decision areas was developed based on the earlier work of Lipham (1974) and the current literature on middle schools. A sample of decision areas that were used in the instrument included the following items:

- Specifying the learning objectives for each unit of instruction
- Setting and revising the goals of the school
- Determining grading procedures for examining the progress of your school
- Allocating materials and equipment to subject, department, or team
- Evaluating how well the subject, department, or team is operating

The entire set of decision areas can be found elsewhere (Barnes, 1994). The current set of 16 items has an alpha coefficient of reliability of .92 and was supported by factor-analytic procedures (Barnes, 1994).

Empirical Findings. We predicted that participation would be positively and significantly related to indicators of quality schools. And indeed, overall effectiveness, openness, health, and student achievement all correlated positively and strongly with our index of teacher participation in schools (the range of *r* was .41 to .66). The correlations are summarized in Table 4.6.

An Index of Strong School Culture

Remember that we posited that if schools were to be successful they must develop a strong shared identity, one that embraces the values of trust, authenticity, cooperation, and shared participation. The empirical results that linked each of these elements of culture with indicators of quality schools supported that proposition. In addition, however, it was assumed that shared identity, trust, authenticity, cooperation, and participation complemented each other, that is, were closely and positively related to each other. We tested this assumption empirically.

First, the five elements of culture were correlated with each other. As can be seen in Panel A of Table 4.7, all the intercorrelations were positive and significant; in fact, most of the correlations were quite substantial, which supported the notion that these elements of culture were complements of each other. Next, to further test this idea, we submitted the data to a principal components factor analysis. One strong factor was identified that explained 59.65% of the variance in the culture elements. All the loadings on this primary factor were .66 or greater (see Panel B of Table 4.7). Our elements of culture come together to form a consistent pattern of culture, one that has a shared identity and is imbued with trust, authenticity, cooperation, and participation.

Because the elements of culture complemented each other and formed a single strong measure of culture, we constructed an index of strong school culture by standardizing the scores on each aspect of culture and then adding them.

Empirical Findings. Not surprisingly, this index of strong school culture also correlated significantly and substantially with teacher openness ($r = .58, p < .01$), principal openness ($r = .62, p < .01$), and health ($r = .67, p < .01$). Moreover, the index was related to student achievement in reading ($r = .42, p < .01$), writing ($r = .44, p < .01$), and mathematics ($r = .45, p < .01$), and strongly related to overall effectiveness ($r = .76, p < .01$).

Conclusion

Strong school cultures have open and healthy school climates. Our analyses also suggested that such schools are generally effective and promote high levels of student achievement in the basic skills of reading, writing, and mathematics.

School Quality

Throughout this chapter the variables that we have examined have been those that we identified in the first chapter as indicators of school quality. Our conception of school quality deals not only with the quality of outcomes but also with the quality of means to achieve those ends. We postulated a set of climate, culture, effectiveness, and student achievement variables that define quality schools. In particular, we conceptualized and measured openness and health

TABLE 4.7 Panel A: Correlations Among Measures of Culture

Variable	Shared Identity	Trust in Principal	Trust in Colleagues	Leader Authenticity	Teacher Authenticity	Cooperation	Participation
Shared identity	1.00	.58**	.39**	.48**	.37**	.36**	.47**
Trust in principal		1.00	.44**	.78**	.45**	.50**	.49**
Trust in colleagues			1.00	.31**	.51**	.76**	.42**
Leader authenticity				1.00	.64**	.49**	.40**
Teacher authenticity					1.00	.83**	.38**
Teacher cooperation						1.00	.45**

Panel B: Factor Loadings of Elements of Culture

Elements of Culture	Factor I
Shared identity	.66
Trust in principal	.80
Trust in colleagues	.75
Leader authenticity	.79
Teacher authenticity	.83
Cooperation	.85
Participation	.70

Factor	Eigenvalue	Percentage of Variance
I	4.17	59.6

**p < .01 (one-tailed tests).

of school climates; student achievement in terms of reading, writing, and mathematics; overall effectiveness in terms of efficiency, flexibility, and adaptability; and a strong school culture with a shared identity that values trust, authenticity, cooperation, and participation.

All the indicators of school quality should form a consistent and complementary pattern. We tested this proposition using a multivariate approach by performing a principal components analysis on our measures of climate openness, school health, school effectiveness, student achievement, and school culture. We hypothesized that all these indicators of school quality would load strongly and highly on a single factor.

Empirical Findings

As predicted, our measures of quality loaded highly on one strong primary factor. All the factor loadings on this school quality factor were greater than .64 and accounted for 56.6% of the variance (see Panel A of Table 4.8). We also did a second analysis in which we included SES as an indicator of quality. The results are quite similar, but a little less variance (55.4%) is explained by the factor (see Panel B of Table 4.8).

Conclusion

The indicators selected for study in our analyses complement each other and seem to tap an underlying characteristic, which we have labeled school quality.

A Parsimonious View of Climate

We have demonstrated that certain aspects of school climate are important contributors, both collectively and independently, to student achievement in middle schools. Features of openness and health create a climate for student success in reading, mathematics, and writing. In particular, when principals are open and nonrestrictive in their behavior (low Restrictiveness) and provide a plethora of teaching resources and materials (Resource Support), they foster a school environment in which teachers set high standards and press

TABLE 4.8 Panel A: Factor Loadings of Quality Indicators
              (SES not included)

Quality Indicators	Factor I
Shared identity	.65
Trust in principal	.73
Trust in colleagues	.71
Leader authenticity	.74
Teacher authenticity	.72
Cooperation	.77
Participation	.76
Overall effectiveness	.83
School health	.89
Principal openness	.78
Teacher openness	.71
Mathematics	.76
Reading	.74
Writing	.71

Factor	Eigenvalue	Percentage of Variance
I	7.92	56.6

Panel B: Factor Loadings of Quality Indicators (SES included)

Quality Indicators	Factor I
Shared identity	.56
Trust in principal	.82
Trust in colleagues	.76
Leader authenticity	.81
Teacher authenticity	.76
Cooperation	.93
Participation	.59
Overall effectiveness	.70
School health	.82
Principal openness	.76
Teacher openness	.62
Mathematics	.94
Reading	.93
Writing	.88
SES	.70

Factor	Eigenvalue	Percentage of Variance
I	4.17	55.4

for achievement (Academic Emphasis), are enthusiastic and like each other (Teacher Affiliation), and treat each other as professional colleagues (Collegial). All of these aspects of climate contribute to the academic achievement of students. The impact of the community also played a role in successful schools. Schools that are confronted by parents and a community that insist on better performance (low Institutional Integrity) have higher achievement levels. Our analyses have examined the separate concepts of openness and health in school climate as they relate individually to student achievement. Now we turn to a combined analysis.

Openness and Health

Open schools tend to be healthy ones, and healthy schools tend to be open. Although the concepts of openness and health are different, there is some overlap in the way each is operationalized. Consequently we examined the intercorrelations among all the dimensions of openness and health as well as SES (see Table 4.9). Because some of the climate variables were highly correlated, we decided to simplify the data for the climate measures before regressing achievement test scores on school climate. Thus, a second-order factor analysis was performed; all 12 aspects of climate openness and health dimensions were factored using a principal components analysis.

Factor-Analytic Results

Using the two criteria of eigenvalue greater than one and simple structure, four factors were identified, which explained 71% of the variance. The rotated factor matrix is summarized in Table 4.10.

Factor I described the relationships between the principal and teachers and is defined by four variables. Supportive and collegial leadership load strongly and positively; directive and restrictive principal behavior load strongly and negatively; hence, we called the factor *Collegial Leadership*, which denotes collegial behavior that is supportive and neither directive nor restrictive.

The second factor described the relationships teachers had with each other. Again four variables load strongly on this factor; teacher commitment, teacher collegiality, and teacher affiliation load in a positive direction and teacher disengagement loads negatively.

TABLE 4.9 Correlations Among Dimensions of Openness, Health, and SES

Variable	DP	RS	CT	CmT	DT	II	CL	PI	RS	AE	TA	SES
Supportive principal	-.55**	.44**	.48**	.36**	-.27*	.15	.82**	.20	.43**	.31**	.45**	.24*
Directive principal		.42**	-.40**	-.30**	.36**	-.15	-.52**	-.27*	-.50**	-.48**	-.48**	-.27*
Restrictive principal			-.28**	-.24*	.10	.16	-.45**	-.03	-.47**	-.45**	-.28**	-.52**
Collegial teacher				.52**	-.25*	.09	.35**	.15	.37**	.25*	.65**	.30**
Committed teacher					-.42**	-.10	.18	.22*	.37**	.36**	.51**	.33**
Disengaged teacher						-.16	-.28**	-.23*	-.31**	-.24*	-.37**	-.18
Institutional integrity							.26*	.21*	.21*	-.09	.09	-.31**
Collegial leadership								.31**	-.45**	.32**	.49**	.17
Principal influence									.39**	.26*	.28**	.17
Resource support										.61**	.52**	.38**
Academic emphasis											.48**	.67**
Teacher affiliation												.38**
DFG (SES)												1.00

NOTE: DP = directive principal, RS = restrictive principal, CT = collegial teacher, CmT = committed teacher, DT = disengaged teacher, II = institutional integrity, CL = collegial leadership, PI = principal influence, RS = resource support, AE = academic emphasis, TA = teacher affiliation.

*p < .05; **p < .01 (two-tailed tests).

TABLE 4.10 Varimax Rotated Factor Matrix: Analysis of Climate Dimensions (N = 86)

Variable	Factor I	Factor II	Factor III	Factor IV
Supportive principal	**.84320**	.31611	.06731	.10102
Directive principal	**−.56522**	−.28692	−.41939	−.07318
Restrictive principal	**−.64022**	−.02591	−.35075	.45962
Collegial teachers	.38348	**.75300**	−.02941	−.07318
Committed teachers	.04167	**.81845**	.22296	−.17213
Disengaged teachers	−.06148	**−.60565**	−.22271	−.26757
Institutional integrity	.19343	−.01704	.01304	**.83903**
Collegial leadership	**.85153**	.14515	.19058	.24357
Resource support	.38200	.25513	**.71132**	.07456
Principal influence	−.01718	.15150	**.64007**	.46898
Teacher affiliation	.34885	**.68448**	.30343	.02764
Academic emphasis	.23698	.21448	**.77303**	−.27214
Eigenvalue	4.87672	1.38214	1.22347	1.04532
Percentage of variance	40.6	11.5	10.2	8.7
Cumulative percentage	40.6	52.1	62.4	71.1

NOTE: Italicized numbers represent the defining factor loadings.

Teachers are committed to students, respect the competence of each other, like each other, and take their work seriously; consequently, we labelled the second factor *Teacher Professionalism*.

Factor III is defined by strong positive loadings of academic emphasis, resource support, and principal influence. This factor is a combination of teachers setting high goals, students responding to the challenge, and the principal supplying the resources and exerting influence on the teachers' behalf; hence, we labeled this factor *Academic Press*.

Finally, the fourth factor is defined by one strong positive variable, institutional integrity. We changed the direction of this scale and called it *Environmental Press*. The change in name was made because first, we wanted to use the notion of press from the inside (academic) and press from the outside (environmental), and second, results of earlier research suggested the construct might be mislabeled (Hannum, Hoy, & Sabo, 1996; Hoy et al., 1991). Changing the name, however, does raise a question about whether this variable is an aspect of school health. Press from the outside does seem to affect student achievement, but such pressure is not positively correlated with the other aspects of health.

Nonetheless, these dimensions of climate capture the essence of both health and openness in a parsimonious manner. Openness of teacher-principal relations is embedded in collegial leadership, and openness of teacher interactions is encapsulated in teacher professionalism. Using the Parsonian framework, all three levels of school organization are examined—the institutional (environmental press), the managerial (collegial leadership), and the technical (teacher professionalism and academic press). Moreover, the perspective calls attention to four important linkages in the school: community-school (environmental press), principal-teacher (collegial leadership), teacher-teacher (teacher professionalism), and teacher-student (academic press).

A Brief Literature Review: A Rationale

Firestone and Wilson (1985) found that principal support was positively related to student learning outcomes, whereas principal control was negatively associated with these outcomes. Similarly, Rosenholtz (1985) concluded from her review of the effective school literature that the principal's supportive actions were a key to effective learning. In brief, principals can influence teaching either by administrative support or control. Support clearly seems more effective than control (Corwin & Borman, 1988); hence, we posited that if the leadership of the principal is to make a difference in terms of student achievement, then it should be collegial leadership.

There is widespread agreement that teacher collegiality is also an important ingredient of improving teacher practice and getting better results (Barth, 1990; Rosenholtz, 1989; Sergiovanni, 1992). Collegial teachers help and support each other, are open to change, and are eager to learn (Johnson, 1990). Collegial teachers trust each other, and it is trust that enables them to try new ideas and take risks. It should not be surprising that a culture of trust is often a key to school effectiveness (Tarter, Sabo, & Hoy, 1995). Moreover, norms of collegiality promote teacher cooperation and collaboration (Little, 1987), attributes that enhance the learning environment and student achievement. Cohesiveness and support, not friction and faultfinding, are teacher characteristics associated with student learning (Anderson & Walberg, 1974; McDill, Meyers, & Rigby, 1967). Moos

(1979) summarized his own research on educational environments by concluding that gains on traditional achievement tests are most likely to occur when there is a combination of warm and supportive relationships, an emphasis on academics, and a well-structured educational environment. Teacher professionalism captures many of the features of teacher-teacher interactions that have been associated with student achievement, for example, strong affiliation with colleagues, commitment to students, and cooperation. Thus, we expected teacher professionalism to be a predictor of student achievement.

There has been some research that has directly examined the relationship between organizational climate and achievement for high schools, but not for middle schools. In general, school health is positively associated with both school effectiveness and student achievement (Hoy et al., 1991) in high schools. The single best organizational climate predictor of student achievement is academic emphasis. High schools with an orderly and serious learning environment, with teachers who set high but achievable goals, and with students who work hard and respect others who do well academically, have higher levels of student achievement, even when data are controlled for socioeconomic status (Hoy et al., 1991). A number of other studies also suggest strong links between academic emphasis and student achievement (Bryk et al., 1993; Murphy et al., 1982; Shouse & Brinson, 1995); consequently, we predicted a strong relationship between academic emphasis and student achievement.

One aspect of climate that is related to student achievement in a surprising way is institutional integrity; it is negatively associated with achievement. In other words, when teachers perceive "interference" in the school from the community, students achieve at higher levels (Hoy et al., 1991). Clearly teachers do not like such interference, but negative consequences in achievement do not ensue; in fact, on the contrary, it seems likely that some press from the community is functional for increased achievement in basic skills. Thus, we concluded that what is important in promoting higher student achievement in schools is an external press from the community for good results, which we label here environmental press.

In summary, supportive and collegial rather than directive and restrictive principal behaviors should be associated with positive student outcomes. Similarly, collegial and affiliative teacher relationships, which foster cooperation and collaboration, should be predictors of higher student achievement. We also posited that internal and external press for achievement have a positive impact on student learning. Academic emphasis is the kind of internal press that produces an atmosphere where there is orderliness and seriousness, where teachers press students to do well academically, and where students accept the challenge for high achievement. Finally, schools with high environmental press are those that feel pressure from the community to improve schooling.

Empirical Findings

To test the hypotheses that elements of health and openness of school climate should be related to student achievement, two statistical procedures were performed. First, correlations were run between the four basic elements of school climate that emerged from the factor analysis and aspects of student achievement. As predicted, school climate was positively associated with student achievement in mathematics, in reading, and in writing; in fact, all four of the elements of health and openness of school climate are significantly correlated with all three measures of student achievement (see Table 4.11). Thus the hypothesized relationships were supported.

One of the problems with nonexperimental research is that it is often difficult to determine the effect of one variable independent of others. This is a special problem for studies that seek to explain the variance of school achievement. Frequently, what seems to be a strong predictor of achievement is merely a proxy for socioeconomic level (SES). Wealthier school districts have higher achievement levels than poorer ones. We deal with this problem in several ways. First, standardized betas and multiple regression coefficients are used to determine the separate and combined contributions of the independent variables, the climate dimensions. Second, all multiple regressions are performed using a set of independent variables that includes SES as well as climate variables. Hence, the independent influence of SES and each climate variable can be determined. Thus, each of the dependent variables was regressed on a set of five variables, which included SES (DFG), collegial leadership, teacher professionalism, academic press, and environmental press.

These multiple regression analyses further clarified the results. For mathematics achievement a multiple R of .85 ($p < .01$) explained 71% of the variance. Environmental press ($\beta = .30, p < .01$), academic

TABLE 4.11 Correlational and Multiple Regression Analysis of Climate Dimensions and SES with Aspects of Student Achievement

Measures of Organizational Climate	Panel A			Panel B		
	Zero-Order Correlations			Measures of Student Achievement Standard Beta Weights		
	Math	Read	Write	Math	Read	Write
Environmental press	.36**	.36**	.35**	.30**	.30**	.30**
Collegial leadership	.48**	.49**	.48**	.13	.19*	.15
Teacher professionalism	.49**	.47**	.49**	.13	.11	.16*
Academic press	.60**	.57**	.57**	.27**	.22**	.24**
SES	.77**	.75**	.73**	.44**	.43**	.40*
Multiple correlation				.85**	.84**	.83**
Adjusted R^2				.71	.68	.66

*$p < .05$; **$p < .01$.

press ($\beta = .27$, $p < .01$), and SES ($\beta = .44$, $p < .01$) all had significant and independent effects on mathematics achievement. For reading achievement, 68% of the variance ($R = .84$, $p < .01$) was explained. Environmental press ($\beta = .30$, $p < .01$), academic press ($\beta = .22$, $p < .01$), collegial leadership ($\beta = .19$, $p < .05$), and SES ($\beta = .43$, $p < .01$) all had significant and independent effects on reading achievement. In writing, 66% of the variance for achievement was explained by the regression equation ($R = .83$, $p < .01$), and environmental press ($\beta = .30$, $p < .01$), teacher professionalism ($\beta = .16$, $p < .05$), academic press ($\beta = .24$, $p < .01$), and SES ($\beta = .40$, $p < .01$) each had a significant independent influence on writing achievement. All the regression analyses are summarized in Panel B of Table 4.11.

Over two thirds of the variance is explained by the independent variables for each of the measures of achievement. All the climate variables make an independent contribution to one or more of the achievement measures. Although socioeconomic status is the single best predictor of achievement, environmental press and academic press are not far behind. Collegial leadership and teacher professionalism work together to contribute to achievement; in fact, if either is omitted from the regression equation, the other makes a significant and independent contribution to the explanation of variance.

Climate and Effectiveness: Climate and Culture

Next, we reexamined the relationship between climate and effectiveness using only the four general aspects of climate and the overall effectiveness index. Except for environmental press ($r = .08$, $p > .05$), all the zero-order correlations between elements of climate and effectiveness were significantly and positively correlated with overall effectiveness ($r = .53$, $.58$, and $.58$ for collegial leadership, teacher professionalism, and academic press, respectively). When overall effectiveness was regressed on these climate dimensions, all the variables made independent and collective contributions to overall effectiveness explaining 48% of the variance ($R = .70$, $p < .01$). The results are summarized in Table 4.12.

Finally, we took another look at culture using our parsimonious measures. Except for environmental press ($r = .03$, $p > .05$), all the zero-order correlations between elements of climate and culture were significantly and positively correlated with our index of strong school culture ($r = .64$, $.62$, and $.56$ for collegial leadership, teacher professionalism, and academic press, respectively). When culture was regressed on these climate elements, they made a collective contribution to culture explaining 50% of the variance ($R = .73$, $p < .01$), but only collegial leadership of the principal and teacher professionalism made unique independent contributions to culture. The results are summarized in Table 4.13.

Conclusion

The organizational climate of middle schools is important for student achievement, especially in the basic skills of reading, writing, and arithmetic. What is the climate profile that facilitates achievement? Environmental press, collegial leadership, teacher professionalism, and academic press are critical ingredients in fostering high academic achievement. Effective middle schools are open and healthy in their interpersonal relationships; they are places where teachers like and respect their colleagues and are committed to their work and students (high teacher professionalism). Teachers see the principal as their ally in the improvement of instruction; the prin-

TABLE 4.12 Correlational and Multiple Regression Analysis of Climate Dimensions and SES with Overall Effectiveness

	Panel A	Panel B (With SES)	
Measures of Organizational Climate	Overall Effectiveness Standard Beta Weights	Overall Effectiveness Standard Beta Weights	Zero-Order r
Environmental press	.17*	.10	.08
Collegial leadership	.21*	.19	.53**
Teacher professionalism	.31**	.29**	.58**
Academic press	.33**	.24*	.58**
SES		.18	.52**
Multiple R	.70**	.71**	
Adjusted R^2	.48**	.48**	

*$p < .05$; **$p < .01$.

cipal is friendly, open, respectful, supportive, and yet establishes and is committed to high standards of teacher performance. There is no need to coerce or restrict teacher behavior; cooperation is freely given by teacher professionals who are committed to teaching and learning (strong collegial leadership). The same pattern of climate characteristics explains the overall effectiveness of schools in this sample. Strong school cultures, however, are determined mostly by the open and healthy principal behavior (strong collegial leadership) and open and healthy teacher behavior (strong teacher professionalism); academic press and environmental press are less important.

General Observations

If there is a surprise in the profile of high achieving schools, it may be the impact of the press that is generated from the outside (environmental press). Although teachers desire buffering from the outside, the data continue to show that overprotection is not functional and may in fact be dysfunctional for high student achievement (Hoy et al., 1991). Pressures from the parents and community seem

TABLE 4.13 Correlational and Multiple Regression Analysis of
Climate Dimensions and SES With Culture

	Panel A	Panel B (With SES)	
Measures of Organizational Climate	Strong Culture Standard Beta Weights	Strong Culture Standard Beta Weights	Zero-Order r
Environmental press	.03	.03	.03
Collegial leadership	.37**	.37**	.64**
Teacher professionalism	.33**	.33**	.62**
Academic press	.16	.17	.56**
SES		.00	.37**
Multiple R	.73**	.73**	
Adjusted R^2	.51**	.50**	

$**p < .01.$

to facilitate rather than hinder. Teachers often view parents as meddling and interfering, but the consequence of such environmental press is positive. Other research (Barth, 1990) similarly suggests that parental involvement increases achievement scores. The RAND studies (Armor et al., 1976) show that simply having parents present in the school helps. Our data support these findings and suggest that, regardless of the rhetoric of the virtues of parental involvement and positive student outcomes, teachers frequently are not overly happy with such involvement because they often see it as interference.

Schools with high student achievement have a strong internal press for academic excellence. Teachers and administrators set a tone that is serious, orderly, and focused on academics. Students respond by accepting the challenge, believing in themselves, and respecting the academic accomplishments of their peers. In the press for achievement, everyone does his or her part. Principals use their influence with superiors to get the necessary resources and support for the instructional program, teachers set reasonable academic goals for their students and go the extra mile in helping them achieve, and students accept the importance of academics and work hard to be successful (high academic press).

The socioeconomic status of the community is always a strong predictor of student achievement; in fact, it typically overwhelms other variables in predicting achievement. This study demonstrates that some climate variables are independently important in explaining achievement. In addition to SES, the variables of environmental press, collegial leadership, teacher professionalism, and academic press are also important, and they are clearly more amenable to intervention and change than SES. Together these aspects of climate, with the possible exception of environmental press, promote an open and healthy school atmosphere that encourages achievement and effectiveness. Commitment (Rosenholtz, 1989), cohesiveness and support (Anderson & Walberg, 1974; McDill et al., 1967), collegial teacher behavior (Barth, 1990; Little, 1987; Rosenholtz, 1989; Sergiovanni, 1992), supportive and collegial principal behavior (Firestone & Wilson, 1985; Moos, 1979), trust (Tarter et al., 1995), and academic emphasis (Bryk et al., 1993; Edmonds, 1979; Moos, 1979) are components of healthy, open, and effective schools and support strong school cultures; in fact, the current findings provide a parsimonious explanation of school-level student achievement.

Our conceptualizations of climate using health and personality metaphors worked well. Health and openness complement each other. Although we reduced the twelve dimensions of the two perspectives to four critical ones, the notions of openness and health were retained. Openness is the general construct that undergirds collegial leadership and teacher professionalism. Health is critical to the connections in the organization—between the school and community, between the principal and teachers, and between teachers and students. This is not surprising because the construct of organizational health was built on Parsons' distinction of levels of organizations—technical, managerial, and institutional. Parsons (1967) himself makes the point that there exist "qualitative breaks" in the line-authority relations at each of the points where the three systems are linked. In service organizations such as schools, another crucial linkage exists between the professionals and clients. Healthy schools are those in which all the linkages are productive. The data of this study suggest that a school need not be completely harmonious to be productive; in fact, a press or dynamic tension that focuses and directs activities may increase productivity. If the internal and external press are directed toward the same goal, then achievement seems to be enhanced, especially if the effort is coupled with openness and cooperation within the system.

Some Implications for Researchers

These findings pose challenges for both researchers and administrators. Although the measures of organizational climate provide a snapshot of school life, climate is a general concept that captures an enduring quality of organizational life (Hoy & Miskel, 1996; Taguiri, 1968). If that is the case, one would expect climate dimensions of schools at a given point to predict achievement for 2 or 3 consecutive years. The following hypothesis should and can be tested with longitudinal achievement data:

H1   Positive relationships between school climate and student achievement will persist over time.

The significance of press for student achievement is intriguing. First, both internal (academic) and external (environmental) press are important. Second, our data suggest that collegiality and cooperation among the professionals in the school transform the pressures from the community (environmental press) into positive actions and attitudes that expect and encourage learning (academic press); that is, collegial leadership and teacher professionalism mediate press. Without collegial relations among the principal and teachers, teachers might respond to the pressures in a much less constructive fashion. Hence, we propose the following hypothesis for testing:

H2   Collegial leadership and teacher professionalism interact with environmental press to produce higher levels of student achievement.

This study examined organizational climate and therefore the unit of analysis was the organization. More than two thirds of the variance in student achievement was explained by the organizational variables of this study; the remaining variance is likely due to individual characteristics of teachers. If in fact teachers translate external pressure into constructive actions with their students, it is also likely that teachers vary in their effectiveness at doing so. One individual characteristic that may be important is teacher efficacy: those teachers who believe that all students can learn and that they can teach them are likely to be more successful in translating pressure (environmental) into positive press (academic). Therefore, we predict that

> H3   Teachers with a high degree of efficacy are more successful translating environmental pressure into academic emphasis than are teachers with a low sense of efficacy (success measured in terms of student achievement).

Of course, this hypothesis awaits further empirical testing, but there is an abundance of evidence that links teacher efficacy to student achievement; in fact, teachers' sense of efficacy is one of the few teacher characteristics consistently related to student achievement (Ashton & Webb, 1986; Moore & Esselman, 1992; Ross, 1992; Ross, Cousins, & Gadalla, 1996) and student affective growth (Borton, 1991; Midgley, Feldlaufer, & Eccles, 1989; Rose & Medway, 1981). In addition, teacher efficacy is associated with other significant outcomes such as teachers' adoption of innovations and use of challenging teaching strategies (Guskey, 1988; Riggs & Enochs, 1990; Ross, 1992; Smylie, 1988; Tracs & Gibson, 1986; Wax & Dutton, 1991), superintendents' ratings of teachers' competence (Trentham, Silvern, & Brogdon, 1985), and teachers' classroom management strategies (Ashton & Webb, 1986; Hoy & Woolfolk, 1990; Woolfolk, Rosoff, & Hoy, 1990). Teacher efficacy is a personal trait, but we find the notion of collective efficacy or school efficacy intriguing. When the teachers in a school as a group believe that they can make a difference, we expect they do. In fact, the health and openness of a school should be related to developing a school sense of efficacy. Consequently, we hypothesize that

> H4   The more open and healthy the school climate, the greater the sense of collective school efficacy.

The present research was concerned with organizational climate and student achievement. Achievement is only one facet of effective schools albeit a highly visible one. Quality schools are also concerned with the social-emotional development of students. Well-adjusted students who are happy, believe in themselves, enjoy school, value education, and respect others are significant school outcomes. The middle school is a crucial link between the self-contained classes of elementary schools and the departmentalization and specialization of most high schools. Student exploration of interests and the healthy social and personal development of adolescents are important features of the middle school. Consequently, as researchers and principals turn to what makes a good middle school, they must be concerned with such expressive outcomes as self-concept, creativity, and citizenship, as well as student achievement in basic skills and higher-level cognitive activities. We offer two hypotheses in this regard:

H5   The more healthy and open the school climate, the less student alienation in the school.

H6   The more healthy and open the school climate, the higher the level of student achievement in higher-level cognitive skills.

For researchers, another important issue is studying and refining the concepts of environmental press and institutional integrity. Some of what seems disruptive to teachers at times has positive consequences for students. We need to sort out destructive and constructive forces. Community involvement in schools does have a contribution to make in improving instructional delivery systems. But not all involvement is helpful; some is counterproductive. Institutional integrity does not differentiate positive forces from negative ones. Simply because teachers do not like interference from the outside does not mean that such efforts are harmful. The finding that environmental press can promote achievement suggests that outside interventions can promote achievement without destroying other healthy interpersonal relationships. Perhaps when the school has healthy interpersonal relationships among students, teachers, and administrators, then challenges from the outside can be made constructive. But when internal interpersonal relations are poor, the same challenges may be destructive. Two research questions are intriguing in this regard:

Q1   Under what conditions does environmental press promote achievement without destroying other healthy interpersonal relationships?

Q2   What are the mechanisms for transforming outside pressure into constructive internal forces?

The concept and measures of organizational climate raise a host of questions concerning structure, motivation, decision making, and communication in schools:

Q3   Are healthy and open school climates prerequisites for school improvement?

Q4   What are the antecedent conditions of open and healthy organizational climates?

Q5   To what extent are the scope and intensity of communications related to school climate?

Q6   Does openness in organizational communication vary with the openness in school climate?

Q7   Does openness in school climate promote openness in formal decision making?

Q8   Does the formal structure of school organizations affect the organizational climate?

Q9   Are teachers more likely to set learning goals rather than performance goals for their students in open and healthy schools?

Q10 Are teachers more likely to believe that student intelligence is improvable rather than fixed in open and healthy schools?

Q11 Are teachers and students more likely to be self-regulated learners in open and healthy schools?

Q12 Are teachers more likely to focus on intrinsic rather than extrinsic motivation in open and healthy schools?

These are only a few examples of the heuristic possibilities that are generated by the climate constructs.

Implications for Administrators

For school administrators the challenge is clear. As we have seen, healthy and open organizational dynamics are important in fostering student achievement. The leadership of the principal may be important, but it is not sufficient in promoting student achievement.

After all, the principal is one step removed from teaching. Collegial leadership that is friendly, supportive, egalitarian, and open is important in providing a sound organizational environment, but it is not enough. Ultimately, only teachers improve instruction; they have to decide they want to improve before it will happen (Hoy & Forsyth, 1986). It is not surprising that collegial leadership and teacher professionalism work together in affecting student achievement. Principals need to find ways to link their leadership efforts with the desires, needs, and efforts of teachers just as teachers must link their efforts with needs and interests of students. Principals also face the challenge of regulating outside forces in a way that produces a dynamic tension for internal operations. They must differentiate between destructive outside forces and constructive external press.

We sketch in broad strokes a few examples of how administrators can use the results of this research.

1. Use the climate framework as an informal guide for analysis and action.

The school climate frameworks allow the administrator to look at school behavior through a set of lenses that underscore important aspects of school life. The nature of the activity in terms of open and authentic relations or the academic emphasis and community press of the school are critical facets that should not go unnoticed. In other words, the climate perspectives provide an easy conceptual guide for analysis and action. One can use the concepts for analysis without engaging in a formal system of measurement.

2. Promote healthy and open school climates because they are both means to ends and ends-in-themselves in the quest for quality.

The instruments can be used in a more formal way. Profiles of climate scores are useful in promoting long-term effectiveness. There is little question that a great many unhealthy and closed school climates exist; our data suggest as much. The climate instruments help pinpoint those aspects of the school workplace that are undesirable and most in need of immediate amelioration. For example, scores on teacher affiliation vary widely from school to school. The usefulness of this empirical measure of the solidarity of the staff is twofold. It describes teachers' perceptions of their relationship with each other in a more systematic way than personal impressions of administrators. And, it places this information within the broader framework of teacher-teacher and teacher-administrator interactions; that is, it is only one element of school climate.

Although the research evidence to date is not abundant, there is beginning to emerge a body of research that suggests strong connections between health, climate, effectiveness, student achievement, and school quality. Open and healthy school climates are an integral part of quality schools. Long-term improvements in academic achievement are connected to a school with strong academic emphasis within the context of a healthy and open environment (Hoy et al., 1991). Not only are health and openness of school climate necessary conditions for effective outcomes, they are desired ends-in-themselves. Thus, a principal might assess the condition of health or climate in a given school and attempt to improve the social context.

3. Use the instruments as the basis for inservice and professional development.

The instruments can be used for inservice and professional development activities for teachers and administrators. The profile of school climate is a picture of the school, but it does not explain causes for the current state of affairs; it simply describes what is. Teachers and administrators who find the profile of their school undesirable must undertake the difficult task of diagnosing the causes of the poor health and then develop strategies for improvement. Successive administrations of the climate instruments can yield a rough measure of the success of the strategies that are employed to improve the school.

4. Improve instructional effectiveness indirectly through the development of an open, healthy, and trusting climate.

The debate between "institutional manager" and "instructional leader" obscures both the leadership and managerial characteristics of the administrative role; that is, no principal is totally an instructional leader, nor is any completely a manager. No principal can afford to be ignorant of the instructional process, yet, ultimately, the principal's role is to create conditions in which teachers operate as autonomous professionals.

To argue that the principal should develop an open and healthy climate is one thing; to do it is another. The interrelationships are complex. For example, the practical difference between supportiveness and directiveness may not be clear. The distinction between principal supportiveness and directiveness depends largely on the extent of teachers' freedom either to accept or to reject the principal's suggestions. This much seems clear: Simply because the principal intends to be supportive by encouraging teachers' freedom does not mean that teachers will interpret these actions as supportive. Furthermore, the principal's avoidance of directive behavior is unlikely to be sufficient to generate a sense of support.

Much of the recent discussion about restructuring schools and school-based management is predicated on the assumption that teachers are professionals, and given the appropriate working conditions and authority, they will make wise decisions in the best interest of the students. Hoy and Forsyth (1986) propose a model of supervision that captures the essence of the independent, yet cooperative nature of improving instruction in schools; the model is based on the assumption that a basic role of the principal is to establish a healthy, open climate.

   5. Assess school health and climate before beginning change
      efforts.

The state of organizational climate will predict the probable success of most change efforts. None of our measures is a quick fix for changing schools, but they can provide a starting point. If we are to change our schools, we need to develop a long-range strategy to improve rather than struggle with a series of more or less inspired short-run change efforts as ends in themselves (Miles, 1969).

Both the OHI-M and the OCDQ-RM provide a snapshot of the state of the school, and both measures yield a diagnosis as well as a baseline from which to judge the effect of change strategies. Our experience demonstrates that a principal's perception of his or her school's climate is frequently at variance with the perceptions of the teachers. To discover such a discrepancy is not to uncover a problem but rather a symptom. The issue is not to determine in some objective sense whether the climate is open or closed, healthy or unhealthy, but to find the root causes for the discrepancy in perceptions. For example, low scores on principal restrictiveness might indicate that the teachers felt that current administrative practice was carried out with too heavy a hand. This is useful information, but it is more useful if the principal can determine the cause of the feelings of restrictiveness. In short, the measures provide a conceptual basis for the diagnosis and solution to many organizational problems.

6. Evaluate your own administrative practice.

We recommend that working school administrators use the health and climate instruments as a continuing assessment of their own administrative practice. The application of either the OHI-M or the OCDQ-RM for formative evaluation is not an unqualified recommendation. The essence of formative evaluation is that it is a continuous guide to the improvement of practice. For a principal, the subtests of the OHI-M and the OCDQ-RM seem to be more appropriate criteria for the evaluation of principal behavior than many of the current standards that masquerade as measures of administrative effectiveness. It is, however, important that there exist a climate of collegiality and trust among administrators if the constructive use of these evaluative tools is to take place. We strongly caution against using any instrument of this kind as summative evaluation. Rather, principals should use these tools for self-evaluation.

In the next chapter, we describe in step-by-step fashion how educators can use the OCDQ-RM and OHI-M to assess and change their schools. Not only are all the instruments, directions, and norms supplied, but we give examples of principals and teachers using the models to improve their schools.

Notes

1. One school in the sample did not complete the OHI-M; hence, in those analyses that involve the health of school climate, the sample size is 86.

2. For a more extensive rationale for this hypothesis, see Hoy and Hannum (1997).

3. The definition and measure of shared identity are based on the work of Price and Mueller (1986).

CHAPTER

5

USING THE OCDQ-RM
AND THE OHI-M:
A PRACTICAL GUIDE
TO ACTION

*There is little point in general models if they do not give
rise to specific conceptual derivations and empirical
applications that illuminate . . . significant day-to-day
practices.*

Jacob W. Getzels, James M. Lipham,
and Roald Campbell, 1968,
Educational Administration as a Social Process

This final chapter is a "how-to-do-it chapter."[1] For both middle
school climate instruments (OCDQ-RM and OHI-M), we review
the conceptual foundations, present the instrument, give directions
for administering and scoring, interpret the results, and illustrate
their use with actual examples. Next, we present a model for chang-

ing school climate, and then the chapter concludes with a practical example using the instruments and change model.

Organizational Climate Description Questionnaire for Middle Schools (OCDQ-RM): Conceptual Foundations

Middle school climate emerges from joint interactions of students, teachers, and administrators. Educators develop collective perceptions of the behavior patterns in their schools. These perceptions, which give the school a distinctive character, are based on the activities, sentiments, and interactions of organizational members. Think of the climate of the school as the school's personality.

The OCDQ-RM describes principal's behavior and teachers' behavior in middle schools. Principal's behavior is examined along three dimensions—the extent to which it is supportive, directive, or restrictive. Supportive behavior is genuine concern and support of teachers. In contrast, directive behavior is starkly task oriented with little concern for the needs of the teachers, and restrictive behavior produces impediments for teachers as they try to do their work.

Likewise, three critical aspects of teacher behavior—collegial, committed, and disengaged— are identified. Collegial behavior supports open and professional interaction among teacher colleagues, and committed teacher behavior is open and helpful to students. On the other hand, disengaged behavior is intolerant and disrespectful; it depicts a general sense of alienation and separation among teachers in school. These fundamental features of principal and teacher behavior are elaborated and summarized as follows:

Principal's Behavior

Supportive behavior is directed toward both the social needs and task achievement of faculty. The principal is helpful, is genuinely concerned with teachers, and attempts to motivate by using constructive criticism and by setting an example through hard work.

Directive behavior is rigid, domineering behavior. The principal maintains close and constant monitoring over virtually all aspects of teacher behavior in the school.

Restrictive behavior hinders rather than facilitates teacher work. The principal burdens teachers with paperwork, committee require- ments, and other demands that interfere with their teaching respon- sibilities.

Teachers' Behavior

Collegial behavior supports open and professional interactions among teachers. Teachers like, respect, and help one another both professionally and personally.

Committed behavior is directed toward helping students to develop both socially and intellectually. Teachers work extra hard to insure student success in school.

Disengaged behavior signifies a lack of meaning and focus in professional activities. Teachers simply are putting in their time; in fact, they are critical and unaccepting of their colleagues.

General Openness
Dimensions

In addition to these six specific dimensions (see Chapter 2), two underlying general aspects of school climate have been identified. The three specific characteristics of principal behavior define a general feature of leader behavior, which is termed openness.

Openness in principal behavior is marked by a helpful concern for the ideas of teachers and constructive support (high supportive- ness), freedom and encouragement for teachers to experiment and act independently (low directiveness), and structuring the routine aspects of the job so that they do not interfere with teaching (low restrictiveness).

Similarly, three specific dimensions of teacher behavior define a second general feature of climate.

Openness in teacher behavior refers to teachers' interactions that are meaningful and tolerant (low disengagement), that help students succeed (high commitment), and that are professional, accepting, and mutually respectful (high collegial relations). The OCDQ-RM, then, provides a description of the school climate in terms of six specific and two general dimensions. That is, each school can be described by mapping its profile along the six dimensions and by computing the openness of the principal and the openness of the faculty.

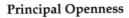

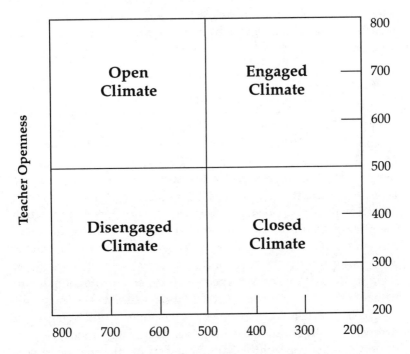

Figure 5.1. Four Types of Middle School Climates

These two general dimensions are relatively independent and are cross partitioned to identify four categories of school climate (see Figure 5.1), which are now defined.

Open Climate

The distinctive features of the open climate are cooperation and respect within the faculty and between the faculty and principal. The principal listens and is receptive to teacher ideas, gives genuine and frequent praise, and respects the competence of faculty (high supportiveness). Principals also give their teachers independence to perform without close scrutiny (low directiveness) and provide facilitating leadership devoid of bureaucratic trivia (low restrictiveness). Likewise, the faculty supports open and professional behavior (high collegial relations) among teachers. Teachers find ways to help students on their own time, if necessary. They are committed to their students and willing to go the extra mile (high commitment). They listen to their colleagues, are respectful, and serious (low disengagement). In brief, the behavior of both the principal and teachers is genuine.

Engaged Climate

The engaged climate is marked, on one hand, by ineffective attempts of the principal to lead, and on the other, by high professional performance of the teachers. The principal is rigid and authoritarian (high directiveness) and respects neither the professional expertise nor personal needs of the faculty (low supportiveness). The principal is seen as burdening faculty with unnecessary busywork (high restrictiveness). Surprisingly, however, the teachers simply ignore the principal's unsuccessful attempts to control and conduct themselves as productive professionals. They respect and support each other, are proud of their school, and enjoy their work (high collegiality). They not only respect each other's professional competence, but they are committed to their students (high commitment). The teachers come together as a cooperative unit engaged and dedicated to the teaching-learning task (high engagement). In brief, the teachers are open with each other and productive in spite of weak principal leadership; the faculty is cohesive, committed, supportive, and engaged.

Disengaged Climate

The disengaged climate stands in stark contrast to the engaged. The principal's leadership behavior is strong, supportive, and concerned. The principal listens to and is open to teachers' views (high supportiveness), gives teachers the freedom to act on the basis of their professional knowledge (low directiveness), and relieves teachers of most of the burdens of paperwork and bureaucratic trivia (low restrictiveness). Nevertheless, the faculty reacts badly; teachers are unwilling to accept responsibility. At best, the faculty simply ignores the initiatives of the principal; at worst, the faculty actively works to immobilize and sabotage the principal's leadership attempts. Teachers not only dislike the principal, but they do not go out of their way to help students (low commitment) and they do not respect each other as colleagues (low collegiality). The faculty is clearly disengaged from its work. Although the principal is open in relationships with faculty, that is, supportive, flexible, and noncontrolling, the faculty is divided, intolerant, uncommitted, and guarded in interactions with each other.

Closed Climate

The closed climate is the antithesis of the open. The principal and teachers simply go through the motions, with the principal stressing routine, trivia, and unnecessary busywork (high restrictiveness) and teachers responding minimally and exhibiting little commitment to the tasks at hand (high disengagement). The principal's leadership is seen as controlling and rigid (high directiveness) as well as unsympathetic and unresponsive (low supportiveness). These misguided tactics are accompanied not only by teacher frustration and apathy but also by suspicion and a lack of faculty respect for colleagues, administrators, and students (low commitment and noncollegiality). In sum, closed climates have principals who are nonsupportive, inflexible, hindering, and controlling, and a faculty that is divided, apathetic, intolerant, and disingenuous. In a word, interactions are closed.

The OCDQ-RM Form

The OCDQ-RM is a 50-item questionnaire on which educators are asked to describe the extent to which specific behavior patterns occur in the school. The responses vary along a 4-point scale defined by the categories *rarely occurs, sometimes occurs, often occurs,* and *very frequently occurs.* The entire instrument as it is administered to teachers is presented in Table 5.1.

Administering the Instrument

The OCDQ-RM is best administered as part of a faculty meeting. It is important to guarantee the anonymity of the teacher respondent; teachers are not asked to sign the questionnaire and no identifying code is placed on the form. Most teachers do not object to responding to the instrument, which takes less than 10 minutes to complete. It is probably advisable to have someone other than the principal in charge

TABLE 5.1 OCDQ-RM

Directions: The following are statements about your school. Please
indicate the extent to which each statement characterizes your
school by circling the appropriate response.

RO = Rarely Occurs   SO = Sometimes Occurs   O = Often Occurs
VFO = Very Frequently Occurs

1. The principal compliments teachers.	RO SO O VFO
2. Teachers have parties for each other.	RO SO O VFO
3. Teachers are burdened with busywork.	RO SO O VFO
4. Routine duties interfere with the job of teaching.	RO SO O VFO
5. Teachers "go the extra mile" with their students.	RO SO O VFO
6. Teachers are committed to helping their students.	RO SO O VFO
7. Teachers help students on their own time.	RO SO O VFO
8. Teachers interrupt other teachers who are talking in staff meetings.	RO SO O VFO
9. The principal rules with an iron fist.	RO SO O VFO
10. The principal encourages teacher autonomy.	RO SO O VFO
11. The principal goes out of his or her way to help teachers.	RO SO O VFO
12. The principal is available after school to help teachers when assistance is needed.	RO SO O VFO
13. Teachers invite other faculty members to visit them at home.	RO SO O VFO
14. Teachers socialize with each other on a regular basis.	RO SO O VFO
15. The principal uses constructive criticism.	RO SO O VFO
16. Teachers who have personal problems receive support from other staff members.	RO SO O VFO
17. Teachers stay after school to tutor students who need help.	RO SO O VFO
18. Teachers accept additional duties if students will benefit.	RO SO O VFO
19. The principal looks out for the personal welfare of the faculty.	RO SO O VFO
20. The principal supervises teachers closely.	RO SO O VFO
21. Teachers leave school immediately after school is over.	RO SO O VFO
22. Most of the teachers here accept the faults of their colleagues.	RO SO O VFO
23. Teachers exert group pressure on nonconforming faculty members.	RO SO O VFO

TABLE 5.1 Continued

24. The principal listens to and accepts teachers' suggestions.	RO SO O VFO
25. Teachers have fun socializing together during school time.	RO SO O VFO
26. Teachers ramble when they talk at faculty meetings.	RO SO O VFO
27. Teachers are rude to other staff members.	RO SO O VFO
28. Teachers make "wise cracks" to each other during meetings.	RO SO O VFO
29. Teachers mock teachers who are different.	RO SO O VFO
30. Teachers don't listen to other teachers.	RO SO O VFO
31. Teachers like to hear gossip about other staff members.	RO SO O VFO
32. The principal treats teachers as equals.	RO SO O VFO
33. The principal corrects teachers' mistakes.	RO SO O VFO
34. Teachers provide strong social support for colleagues.	RO SO O VFO
35. Teachers respect the professional competence of their colleagues.	RO SO O VFO
36. The principal goes out of his or her way to show appreciation to teachers.	RO SO O VFO
37. The principal keeps a close check on sign-in times.	RO SO O VFO
38. The principal monitors everything teachers do.	RO SO O VFO
39. Administrative paperwork is burdensome at this school.	RO SO O VFO
40. Teachers help and support each other.	RO SO O VFO
41. The principal closely checks teacher activities.	RO SO O VFO
42. Assigned nonteaching duties are excessive.	RO SO O VFO
43. The interactions between team/unit members are cooperative.	RO SO O VFO
44. The principal accepts and implements ideas suggested by faculty members.	RO SO O VFO
45. Members of teams/units consider other members to be their friends.	RO SO O VFO
46. Extra help is available to students who need help.	RO SO O VFO
47. Teachers volunteer to sponsor after-school activities.	RO SO O VFO
48. Teachers spend time after school with students who have individual problems.	RO SO O VFO
49. The principal sets an example by working hard himself or herself.	RO SO O VFO
50. Teachers are polite to one another.	RO SO O VFO

SOURCE: Hoffman (1993).

of collecting the data. It is important to create a nonthreatening atmosphere in which teachers give candid responses. All of the health and climate instruments follow this same protocol for administration.

The Subscales

The 50 items of the instrument define the six dimensions of the OCDQ-RM. The specific items, which provide the operational scales for each dimension, are presented in Table 5.2.

The items are scored by assigning 1 to *rarely occurs*, 2 to *sometimes occurs*, 3 to *often occurs*, and 4 to *very frequently occurs*. When an item is reverse scored (indicated by an asterisk in Table 5.2), *rarely occurs* receives a 4, *sometimes occurs* a 3, and so on. Each item is scored for each respondent, and then an average school score for each item is computed by averaging the item responses across the school; remember, the school is the unit of analysis. For example, if School A has 25 teachers responding to the OCDQ-RM, each individual questionnaire is scored and then an average score for all respondents is computed for each item. Thus, the average score for the 25 teachers is calculated for Item 1 and then Item 2 and so on. The average school scores for the items defining each subtest are added to yield school subtest scores. The six subtest scores represent the climate profile for the school.

Scoring the OCDQ-RM

Step 1: Score each item for each respondent with the appropriate number (1, 2, 3, or 4). Be sure to reverse score items 21 and 50.

Step 2: Calculate an average school score for each item. For each item, add all the teachers' scores who responded and then divide by the number of teachers. In the previous example, one would add all 25 teacher scores for each item and then divide the sum by 25. Round the scores to the nearest hundredth. This score represents the average school item score. You should have 50 average school item scores before proceeding.

TABLE 5.2 The Items That Compose the Six Subtests of the
OCDQ-RM

Principal's Behavior

Supportive behavior items	*Questionnaire number*
1. The principal compliments teachers.	(1)
2. The principal encourages teacher autonomy.	(10)
3. The principal goes out of his or her way to help teachers.	(11)
4. The principal is available after school to help teachers when assistance is needed.	(12)
5. The principal uses constructive criticism.	(15)
6. The principal looks out for the personal welfare of the faculty.	(19)
7. The principal listens to and accepts teachers' suggestions.	(24)
8. The principal treats teachers as equals.	(32)
9. The principal goes out of his or her way to show appreciation to teachers.	(36)
10. The principal accepts and implements ideas suggested by faculty members.	(44)
11. The principal sets an example by working hard himself or herself.	(49)

Directive behavior items	*Questionnaire number*
1. The principal rules with an iron fist.	(9)
2. The principal supervises teachers closely.	(20)
3. The principal corrects teachers' mistakes.	(33)
4. The principal keeps a close check on sign-in times.	(37)
5. The principal monitors everything teachers do.	(38)
6. The principal closely checks teacher activities.	(41)

Restrictive behavior items	*Questionnaire number*
1. Teachers are burdened with busywork.	(3)
2. Routine duties interfere with the job of teaching.	(4)
3. Administrative paperwork is burdensome at this school.	(39)
4. Assigned nonteaching duties are excessive.	(42)

(Continued)

TABLE 5.2 Continued

Teachers' Behavior

Collegial behavior items	*Questionnaire number*
1. Teachers have parties for each other.	(2)
2. Teachers invite other faculty members to visit them at home.	(13)
3. Teachers socialize with each other on a regular basis.	(14)
4. Teachers who have personal problems receive support from other staff members.	(16)
5. Most of the teachers here accept the faults of their colleagues.	(22)
6. Teachers have fun socializing together during school time.	(25)
7. Teachers provide strong social support for colleagues.	(34)
8. Teachers respect the professional competence of their colleagues.	(35)
9. Teachers help and support each other.	(40)
10. The interactions between team/unit members are cooperative.	(43)
11. Members of teams/units consider other members to be their friends.	(45)

Committed behavior items	*Questionnaire number*
1. Teachers "go the extra mile" with their students.	(5)
2. Teachers are committed to helping their students.	(6)
3. Teachers help students on their own time.	(7)
4. Teachers stay after school to tutor students who need help.	(17)

Step 3: Sum the average school item scores as follows:

Supportive behavior (S) = 1 + 10 + 11 + 12 + 15 + 19 +24 + 32 + 36 + 44 + 49

Directive behavior (D) = 9 + 20 + 33 + 37 + 38 + 41

Restrictive behavior (R) = 3 + 4 + 39 + 42

Collegial behavior (C) = 2 + 13 + 14 + 16 + 22 + 25 + 34 + 35 + 40 + 43 + 45

TABLE 5.2 Continued

Teachers' Behavior

Committed behavior items	*Questionnaire number*
5. Teachers accept additional duties if students will benefit.	(18)
*6. Teachers leave school immediately after school is over.	(21)
7. Extra help is available to students who need help.	(46)
8. Teachers volunteer to sponsor after-school activities.	(47)
9. Teachers spend time after school with students who have individual problems.	(48)

Disengaged behavior items	*Questionnaire number*
1. Teachers interrupt other teachers who are talking in staff meetings.	(8)
2. Teachers exert group pressure on nonconforming faculty members.	(23)
3. Teachers ramble when they talk at faculty meetings.	(26)
4. Teachers are rude to other staff members.	(27)
5. Teachers make "wise cracks" to each other during meetings.	(28)
6. Teachers mock teachers who are different.	(29)
7. Teachers don't listen to other teachers.	(30)
8. Teachers like to hear gossip about other staff members.	(31)
*9. Teachers are polite to one another.	(50)

* = scored in reverse.

Committed behavior (Com) = 5 + 6 + 7 + 17 + 18 + 21 + 46 + 47 + 48

Disengaged behavior (Dis) = 8 + 23 + 26 + 27 + 28 + 29 + 30 + 31 + 50

These six scores represent the climate profile of the school. You may wish to compare your school profile with other schools. You must convert each school score to a standardized score. The current database on middle schools is drawn from a large, diverse sample of schools from New Jersey. The average scores and standard deviations for each climate dimension are summarized as follows:

	Mean *(M)*	*Standard Deviation* *(SD)*
Supportive behavior (S)	29.39	4.61
Directive behavior (D)	12.09	2.40
Restrictive behavior (R)	9.11	1.52
Collegial behavior (C)	29.30	3.01
Committed behavior (Com)	26.76	2.74
Disengaged behavior (Dis)	15.56	2.18

Computing Standardized Score of the OCDQ-RM

Convert the school subtest scores to standardized scores with a mean of 500 and a standard deviation of 100, which we call SdS scores. Use the following formulas:

SdS for S = $100(S - 29.39)/4.61 + 500$

First compute the difference between your school score on S and the mean of 29.39 for the normative sample (S – 29.39). Then multiply the difference by 100 [100(S – 29.39)]. Next divide the product by standard deviation of the normative sample (4.61). Then add 500 to the result. You have computed a standardized score (SdS) for the supportive behavior sub-scale (S).

Repeat the process for each dimension as follows:

SdS for D = $100(D - 12.09)/2.40 + 500$
SdS for R = $100(R - 9.11)/1.52 + 500$
SdS for C = $100(C - 29.30)/3.01 + 500$
SdS for Com = $100(Com - 26.76)/2.74 + 500$
SdS for Dis = $100(Dis - 15.56)/2.18 + 500$

You have standardized your school scores against the normative data provided in the New Jersey sample. For example, if your school score is 600 on supportive behavior, it is one standard deviation above the average score on supportive behavior of all schools in the sample; that is, the principal is more supportive than 84% of the other principals. A score of 300 represents a school that is two standard deviations below the mean on the subtest. You may recognize this system as the one used in reporting individual scores on the SAT, CEEB, and GRE.

There are two other scores that can be easily computed and are usually of interest to teachers and principals. Accordingly, the two openness measures can be computed as follows:

$$\text{Principal Openness} = \frac{(\text{SdS for S}) + (1000 - \text{SdS for D}) + (1000 - \text{SdS for R})}{3}$$

$$\text{Teacher Openness} = \frac{(\text{SdS for C}) + (\text{SdS for Com}) + (1000 - \text{SdS for Dis})}{3}$$

These openness indexes are interpreted the same way as the subtest scores; that is, the mean of the "average" school is 500. Thus, a score of 650 on teacher openness represents a highly open faculty, one that is one and a half standard deviations above the average school.

Prototypic profiles of climates have been constructed using the normative data from the New Jersey sample of middle schools (see Table 5.3). Therefore, you can examine the fit of your own school climate to the four prototypes. Compare the standardized scores of your school with each of the prototypes in Table 5.3 to determine which of the four climate types the school most closely resembles. Note that a given school can be described by one or two indexes. A total score of 1,150 or more is almost certain to be the mark of a school with an open climate. By the same token, a school with a score below 850 will have a closed climate. Most school scores, however, fall between these extremes and can only be diagnosed by carefully comparing all elements of the climate with the four prototypes. We recommend using all six dimensions of OCDQ-RM to gain a finely tuned picture of school climate.

An Actual Example

Recently, we assessed the climates of middle schools. The OCDQ-RM was administered to the teachers at faculty meetings. The data were then returned to us, and using the procedures described above, we scored and analyzed the climate openness of the schools. School data can be scored by our computer program, which includes a comparison of your school with the normative sample and classifies the climate.[2] Two of the schools, Wilson and Frost, serve as our examples.[3]

TABLE 5.3 Prototypic Profiles of Middle School Climate Types

Climate Dimension	Open Climate	Engaged Climate	Disengaged Climate	Closed Climate
Supportive	618 (VH)	376 (VL)	553 (H)	393 (VL)
Directive	394 (VL)	591 (H)	444 (L)	606 (VH)
Restrictive	425 (L)	551 (H)	437 (L)	624 (VH)
Collegial	604 (VH)	635 (VH)	450 (L)	371 (VL)
Committed	622 (VH)	588 (H)	411 (L)	421 (L)
Disengaged	409 (L)	442 (L)	587 (H)	594 (H)
Principal Openness	600 (H)	411 (L)	557 (H)	388 (VL)
Teacher Openness	606 (VH)	594 (H)	425 (L)	399 (VL)
Total	1,206	1,005	982	787

NOTE: VH = very high; H = High; VL = very low; L = low.

The scores have been standardized so that the average score for a middle school in the sample is 500 and the standard deviation is 100. We have done this for two reasons. First, the scores are easily compared with others in the sample; and second, their interpretation is not unlike that of SAT scores, scores with which most teachers and administrators are familiar. For example, a score of 600 on the Supportive Principal Behavior scale is one standard deviation above all the schools in the sample, a relatively high score. Similarly, a score of 500 represents a school that is average in comparison to others, while a 400 indicates a school one standard deviation below the average school scores, a relatively low score. We have changed the numbers into categories ranging from high to low by using the following conversion table:

Above 550	HIGH
525-550	ABOVE AVERAGE
511-524	SLIGHTLY ABOVE AVERAGE
490-510	AVERAGE
476-489	SLIGHTLY BELOW AVERAGE
450-475	BELOW AVERAGE
Below 450	LOW

The climate-openness profiles for Wilson and Frost and a brief sketch of the climate of each school are given next. We begin with a climate profile for Wilson Middle School. The six subtest scores and two openness scores were computed using the formulas to standardize the scores just described.

The climate of Wilson Middle School is open (see Figure 5.2). Teachers are highly professional in their interactions with each other and respect the work of their colleagues (high on collegiality). They also demonstrate a strong commitment to students (high on commitment); they are willing to go the extra mile in helping students achieve. Teachers are typically tolerant and engaged in meaningful professional activities (low disengagement). There is also substantial openness of the principal's behavior (high). The principal is more supportive of teachers than most middle school principals (high on supportive behavior). Moreover, the principal neither controls teachers tightly nor monitors their actions closely, but rather gives them considerable autonomy (low directive behavior). Finally, the principal facilitates teacher activity by not burdening them with busywork or other administrative trivia that shift their attention from the teaching-learning process (low restrictive behavior). In brief, both the behavior of the principal and teachers is open.

Let's examine Figure 5.3, the climate-openness profile of Frost Middle School, one of the most closed climates that we have encountered. The principal does not support the teachers (low supportive behavior); rather, this principal spends most of the time ordering people around and watching them carefully (high directive behavior). Such close supervision is complemented by a mountain of paperwork and administrative trivia (high restrictive behavior). Teachers are not engaged in productive group efforts with either the principal or other faculty members (high disengagement). Moreover, they are not particularly accessible to students; they don't volunteer extra effort and they don't go out of their way to help students (low committed behavior). Similarly, they don't like and support each other (low collegial behavior). This is not a good place for teachers or students. In a word, it is closed.

The contrast between these two schools is startling. Wilson is a good place to work. The principal's leadership is enlightened, and faculty members respond as professionals; they are committed to the task at hand and supportive of each other as well as the principal. The interpersonal relationships are genuine. When the principal does criticize, it is for a constructive purpose and the teachers accept

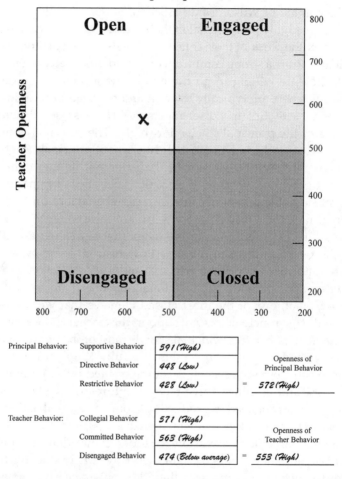

Figure 5.2. Organizational Climate Description Questionnaire for Middle Schools (OCDQ-RM)

that. This is not a school to be tinkered with; the work environment complements the teaching-learning task.

Frost, by comparison, is a dismal place to teach or to practice administration. Suspicion and turmoil pervade the halls and classrooms of this school. Attempts by the principal to lead are directive,

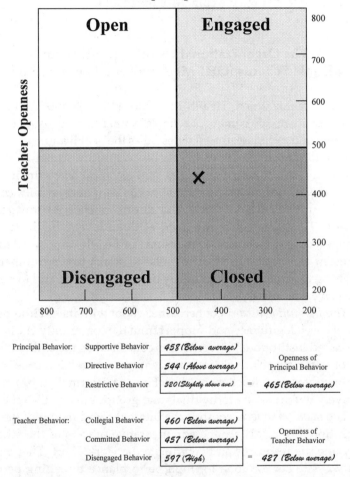

Figure 5.3. Organizational Climate Description Questionnaire for Middle Schools (OCDQ-RM)

restrictive, and ineffective. The principal is not there to be supportive. Rules, regulations, and busywork are substitutes for active educational leadership. Teachers respond by disengaging from the collective task. They are not friendly with each other, and they don't support each other. The students lose out also. Teachers not only don't enjoy their colleagues or administrators, but they have little time for students. There is no quick fix here, but it is in everyone's best interest to change the climate of the school.

The Organizational Health Inventory for Middle Schools (OHI-M): Conceptual Foundations

The Organizational Health Inventory (OHI) is another instrument to evaluate the climate of schools. Rather than focusing on the openness of the climate, the OHI describes the health and well-being of behavior and interactions in schools. A healthy school is one in which the institutional, managerial, and technical levels are in harmony; the school meets functional needs as it successfully copes with disruptive external forces and directs its energies toward its mission. Health is conceptualized at three levels: institutional, managerial, and technical. Dimensions of health were selected to represent the basic needs of schools: to adapt to environmental demands, to achieve goals, to satisfy participant needs, and to create a cohesive community.

The *institutional level* connects the school with its environment. Schools need legitimacy and support from the community. A dimension called institutional integrity was conceived as the ability of the school to remain relatively independent from vested interests. Both administrators and teachers need backing to perform their functions relatively unfettered by individuals and groups outside the school.

The *managerial level* controls the internal coordination of the organization; principals are the administrative officers of the school. They allocate resources and coordinate the work effort. They must find ways to set the tone for high performance by letting people know what is expected of them in ways that are friendly and guided by professionalism. Principal influence and resource support are basic leadership activities that insure the presence of adequate instructional materials and resources requested by teachers.

The *technical level* of the school is concerned with the teaching-learning process. The primary function of the school is to produce educated students. Moreover, teachers and supervisors have immediate responsibility for solving the problems associated with effective learning and teaching. Teacher affiliation, a key mechanism for integrating school life, reflects a cohesive work unit that is committed equally to colleagues and students. Academic emphasis, the school's press for achievement, is the setting of high but achievable student goals and a dedication of both students and teachers to academic excellence. These fundamental features of school health are summarized as follows:

Institutional Level

Institutional Integrity is the degree to which the school can cope with its environment in a way that maintains the educational integrity of its programs. Teachers are protected from unreasonable community and parental demands.

Managerial Level

Collegial Leadership is principal behavior that is friendly, supportive, open, and guided by norms of equality. But, at the same time, the principal sets the tone for high performance by letting people know what is expected of them.

Principal Influence is the principal's ability to influence the actions of superiors. Influential principals are persuasive with superiors, get additional consideration, and proceed relatively unimpeded by the hierarchy.

Resource Support is the extent to which classroom supplies and instructional materials are readily available; in fact, even extra materials are supplied if requested.

Technical Level

Teacher Affiliation is a sense of friendliness and strong association with the school. Teachers feel good about each other, their job, and their students. They are committed to both their students and their colleagues and accomplish their jobs with enthusiasm.

Academic Emphasis is the extent to which the school is driven by a quest for academic excellence. High but achievable academic goals are set for students; the learning environment is orderly and serious; teachers believe in their students' ability to achieve; students work hard and respect those who do well academically.

A healthy school is one in which the teacher, administrative, and institutional levels are in harmony. The school meets its needs of adaptation, goal achievement, participant satisfaction, and group cohesiveness as it successfully copes with disruptive external forces and continues its mission. School health captures the positive contribution of all six dimensions. Brief vignettes of the healthy and sick school are now described.

Healthy School

Student, teacher, and principal behavior are harmonious in healthy schools. Teachers like their colleagues, their school, their job, and their students (high teacher affiliation), and they are driven by a quest for academic excellence. Teachers believe in themselves and their students; consequently, they set high but achievable goals. The learning environment is serious and orderly, and students work hard and respect others who do well academically (high academic emphasis). Principal behavior is also healthy, that is, friendly, open, egalitarian, and supportive. Such principals expect the best from teachers (high collegial leadership). Principals get teachers the resources they need to do the job (high resource support) and are also influential with superiors (high principal influence); they go to bat for their teachers. Finally, a healthy school has high institutional integrity; teachers are protected from unreasonable and hostile outside forces.

Unhealthy School

An unhealthy school is vulnerable to destructive outside forces. Teachers and administrators are bombarded by parental demands (low institutional integrity). The school is without an effective principal. The principal provides little direction or structure and exhibits scant encouragement for teachers (low collegial leadership), and has negligible clout with superiors (low principal influence). Teachers don't especially like their colleagues or their jobs. They act aloof, suspicious, and defensive (low teacher affiliation). Instructional materials, supplies, and supplementary materials are not available when needed (low resource support). Finally, there is minimal press for academic excellence. Neither teachers nor students take academic life seriously; in fact, academically oriented students are ridiculed by their peers and viewed by their teachers as threats (low academic emphasis).

The OHI-M Form

The OHI-M is a 45-item questionnaire on which educators are asked to describe the extent to which specific behavior patterns occur in the school. The responses vary along a 4-point scale defined by the categories *rarely occurs, sometimes occurs, often occurs,* and *very frequently occurs.* The entire instrument as it is administered to teachers is presented in Table 5.4.

Administering the Instrument

The OHI-M is best administered as part of a faculty meeting. It is important to guarantee the anonymity of the teacher respondent; teachers are not asked to sign the questionnaire and no identifying code is placed on the form. Most teachers do not object to responding to the instrument, which takes less than 10 minutes to complete. We recommend that someone other than an administrator collect the data. It is important to create a nonthreatening atmosphere in which teachers give candid responses. All of the health instruments follow the same pattern of administration.

The Subscales

After the 45-item instrument is administered to the faculty, the items for each scale are scored. The items for each scale are presented in Table 5.5.

The items are scored by assigning 1 to *rarely occurs,* 2 to *sometimes occurs,* 3 to *often occurs,* and 4 to *very frequently occurs.* When an item is reverse scored (noted by an asterisk in Table 5.5), *rarely occurs* receives a 4, *sometimes occurs* a 3, and so on. Each item is scored for each respondent, and then an average school score for each item is computed by averaging the item responses across the school; remember, the school is the unit of analysis. The average school scores for the items comprising each subtest are added to yield school subtest scores. The six subtest scores represent the health profile for the school. For example, if School A has 50 teachers responding to the OHI-M, each individual questionnaire is scored and then an average score for all respondents is computed for each item. Thus, the average score for the 50 teachers is calculated for Item 1 and then Item 2 and so on. The average school scores for the items

(Text continues on p. 150)

TABLE 5.4 OHI-M

Directions: The following are statements about your school. Please indicate the extent to which each statement characterizes your school by circling the appropriate response.

*RO = Rarely Occurs   SO = Sometimes Occurs   O = Often Occurs
VFO = Very Frequently Occurs*

1. The principal explores all sides of topics and admits that other options exist.	RO	SO	O	VFO
2. Students make provisions to acquire extra help from teachers.	RO	SO	O	VFO
3. The principal gets what he or she asks for from superiors.	RO	SO	O	VFO
4. The principal discusses classroom issues with teachers.	RO	SO	O	VFO
5. The principal accepts questions without appearing to snub or quash the teacher.	RO	SO	O	VFO
6. Extra materials are available if requested.	RO	SO	O	VFO
7. Students neglect to complete homework.	RO	SO	O	VFO
8. The school is vulnerable to outside pressures.	RO	SO	O	VFO
9. The principal is able to influence the actions of his or her superiors.	RO	SO	O	VFO
10. The principal treats all faculty members as his or her equal.	RO	SO	O	VFO
11. Teachers are provided with adequate materials for their classrooms.	RO	SO	O	VFO
12. Teachers in this school like each other.	RO	SO	O	VFO
13. Community demands are accepted even when they are not consistent with the educational program.	RO	SO	O	VFO
14. The principal lets faculty know what is expected of them.	RO	SO	O	VFO
15. Teachers receive necessary classroom supplies.	RO	SO	O	VFO
16. Students respect others who get good grades.	RO	SO	O	VFO
17. Good grades are important to the students of this school.	RO	SO	O	VFO
18. Teachers feel pressure from the community.	RO	SO	O	VFO
19. The principal's recommendations are given serious consideration by his or her superiors.	RO	SO	O	VFO
20. Supplementary materials are available for classroom use.	RO	SO	O	VFO
21. Teachers exhibit friendliness to each other.	RO	SO	O	VFO
22. Students seek extra work so they can get good grades.	RO	SO	O	VFO

TABLE 5.4 Continued

23. Select citizen groups are influential with the board.	RO	SO	O	VFO
24. The principal looks out for the personal welfare of faculty members.	RO	SO	O	VFO
25. The school is open to the whims of the public.	RO	SO	O	VFO
26. A few vocal parents can change school policy.	RO	SO	O	VFO
27. Students try hard to improve on previous work.	RO	SO	O	VFO
28. Teachers accomplish their jobs with enthusiasm.	RO	SO	O	VFO
29. The learning environment is orderly and serious.	RO	SO	O	VFO
30. The principal is friendly and approachable.	RO	SO	O	VFO
31. Teachers show commitment to their students.	RO	SO	O	VFO
32. Teachers are indifferent to each other.	RO	SO	O	VFO
33. Teachers are protected from unreasonable community and parental demands.	RO	SO	O	VFO
34. The principal is able to work well with the superintendent.	RO	SO	O	VFO
35. The principal is willing to make changes.	RO	SO	O	VFO
36. Teachers have access to needed instructional materials.	RO	SO	O	VFO
37. Teachers in this school are cool and aloof to each other.	RO	SO	O	VFO
38. Teachers in this school believe that their students have the ability to achieve academically.	RO	SO	O	VFO
39. The principal is understanding when personal concerns cause teachers to arrive late or leave early.	RO	SO	O	VFO
40. Our school gets its fair share of resources from the district.	RO	SO	O	VFO
41. The principal is rebuffed by the superintendent.	RO	SO	O	VFO
42. Teachers volunteer to help each other.	RO	SO	O	VFO
43. The principal is effective in securing the superintendent's approval for new programs or activities.	RO	SO	O	VFO
44. Academically oriented students in this school are ridiculed by their peers.	RO	SO	O	VFO
45. Teachers do favors for each other.	RO	SO	O	VFO

SOURCE: Barnes (1994).

TABLE 5.5 The Items That Compose the Seven Subtests of the OHI

Institutional Level

Institutional integrity items	*Questionnaire number*
*1. The school is vulnerable to outside pressures.	(8)
*2. Community demands are accepted even when they are not consistent with the educational program.	(13)
*3. Teachers feel pressure from the community.	(18)
*4. Select citizen groups are influential with the board.	(23)
*5. The school is open to the whims of the public.	(25)
*6. A few vocal parents can change school policy.	(26)
7. Teachers are protected from unreasonable community and parental demands.	(33)

Administrative Level

Collegial leadership items	*Questionnaire number*
1. The principal explores all sides of topics and admits that other opinions exist.	(1)
2. The principal discusses classroom issues with teachers.	(4)
3. The principal accepts questions without appearing to snub or quash the teacher.	(5)
4. The principal treats all faculty members as his or her equal.	(10)
5. The principal lets faculty know what is expected of them.	(14)
6. The principal looks out for the personal welfare of faculty members.	(24)
7. The principal is friendly and approachable.	(30)
8. The principal is willing to make changes.	(35)
9. The principal is understanding when personal concerns cause teachers to arrive late or leave early.	(39)

Principal influence items	*Questionnaire number*
1. The principal gets what he or she asks for from superiors.	(3)
2. The principal is able to influence the actions of his or her superiors.	(9)
3. The principal's recommendations are given serious consideration by his or her superiors.	(19)

TABLE 5.5 Continued

Administrative Level

Principal influence items	*Questionnaire number*
4. The principal is able to work well with the superintendent.	(34)
*5. The principal is rebuffed by the superintendent.	(41)
6. The principal is effective in securing the superintendent's approval for new programs and activities.	(43)

Resource support items	*Questionnaire number*
1. Extra materials are available if requested.	(6)
2. Teachers are provided with adequate materials for their classrooms.	(11)
3. Teachers receive necessary classroom supplies.	(15)
4. Supplementary materials are available for classroom use.	(20)
5. Teachers have access to instructional material.	(36)
6. Our school gets its fair share of resources from the district.	(40)

Teacher Level

Teacher affiliation items	*Questionnaire number*
1. Teachers in the school like each other.	(12)
2. Teachers exhibit friendliness to each other.	(21)
3. Teachers accomplish their jobs with enthusiasm.	(28)
4. Teachers show commitment to their students.	(31)
*5. Teachers are indifferent to each other.	(32)
*6. Teachers in this school are cool and aloof to each other.	(37)
7. Teachers volunteer to help each other.	(42)
8. Teachers do favors for each other.	(45)

Academic emphasis items	*Questionnaire number*
1. Students make provisions to acquire extra help from teachers.	(2)
*2. Students neglect to complete homework.	(7)

(Continued)

TABLE 5.5 Continued

Teacher Level *Academic emphasis items*	*Questionnaire number*
3. Students respect others who get good grades.	(16)
4. Good grades are important to the students of this school.	(17)
5. Students seek extra help so they can get good grades.	(22)
6. Students try hard to improve on previous work.	(27)
7. The learning environment is orderly and serious.	(29)
8. Teachers in this school believe that their students have the ability to achieve academically.	(38)
*9. Academically oriented students in this school are ridiculed by their peers.	(44)

* = scored in reverse.

defining each subtest are added to yield school subtest scores. The six subtest scores represent the health profile for the school.

Scoring the OHI-M

Step 1: Score each item for each respondent with the appropriate number (1, 2, 3, or 4). Be sure to reverse score items 7, 8, 13, 18, 23, 25, 26, 32, 37, 41, and 44.

Step 2: Calculate an average school score for each item. In the previous example, one would add all 50 scores on each item and then divide the sum by 50. Round the scores to the nearest hundredth. This score represents the average school item score. You should have 45 school item scores before proceeding.

Step 3: Sum the average school item scores as follows:
Institutional Integrity (II) = 8 + 13 + 18 + 23 + 25 + 26 + 33
Collegial Leadership (CL) = 1 + 4 + 5 + 10 + 14 + 24 + 30 + 35 + 39
Principal Influence (PI) = 3 + 9 + 19 + 34 + 41 + 43
Resource Support (RS) = 6 + 11 + 15 + 20 + 36 + 40
Teacher Affiliation (TA) = 12 + 21 + 28 + 31 + 32 + 37 + 42 + 45

Academic Emphasis (AE) = 2 + 7 + 16 + 17 + 22 + 27 + 29 + 38 + 44

These six scores represent the health profile of the school. You may wish to compare your school profile with other schools. To do so, we recommend that you standardize each school score. The current data base on middle schools is drawn from a large, diverse sample of schools from New Jersey. The average scores and standard deviations for each health dimension are summarized below:

	Mean (M)	Standard Deviation (SD)
Institutional Integrity (II)	16.41	2.82
Collegial Leadership (CL)	26.61	3.71
Principal Influence (PI)	16.37	2.12
Resource Support (RS)	16.72	2.63
Teacher Affiliation (TA)	28.34	2.57
Academic Emphasis (AE)	20.11	2.80

Computing the Standardized Scores for the OHI-M

Convert the school subtest scores to standardized scores with a mean of 500 and a standard deviation of 100, which we call SdS score. Use the following formulas:

SdS for II = $100(II - 16.41)/2.82 + 500$

First compute the difference between your school score on II and the mean for the normative sample $(II - 16.41)$. Then multiply the difference by 100 $[100(II - 16.41)]$. Next divide the product by the standard deviation of the normative sample (2.82). Then add 500 to the result. You have computed a standardized score (SdS) for the institutional integrity subscale.

Repeat the process for each dimension as follows:

SdS for CL = $100(CL - 26.61)/3.71 + 500$
SdS for PI = $100(PI - 16.37)/2.12 + 500$
SdS for RS = $100(RS - 16.72)/2.63 + 500$

$$\text{SdS for TA} = 100(\text{TA} - 28.34)/2.57 + 500$$
$$\text{SdS for AE} = 100(\text{AE} - 20.11)/2.80 + 500$$

You have standardized your school scores against the normative data provided in the New Jersey sample. For example, if your school score is 700 on institutional integrity, it is two standard deviations above the average score on institutional integrity of all schools in the sample; that is, the school has more institutional integrity than 97% of the schools in the sample.

An overall index of school health can be computed as follows:

$$\text{Health} = \frac{(\text{SdS for II}) + (\text{Sds for CL}) + (\text{SdS for PI}) + (\text{SdS for RS}) + (\text{SdS for TA}) + (\text{SdS for AE})}{6}$$

This health index is interpreted the same way as the subtest scores; that is, the mean of the "average" school is 500. Thus, a score of 650 on the health index represents a very healthy school, one that is one and a half standard deviations above the average school. A score of 350 represents a school with a very sick climate. Most school scores, however, fall between these extremes and can only be diagnosed by carefully comparing all elements of the climate with the four prototypes.

Prototypic profiles for healthy and unhealthy schools have been constructed using the normative data from the New Jersey sample of middle schools (see Table 5.6). Here one can examine the fit of one's own school to the contrasting prototypes. An overall health index of 650 or more is almost certain to be the mark of a healthy school. We recommend using all six dimensions of the OHI-M to gain a finely tuned picture of school health.

An Example

We assessed the climate of Wilson Middle School earlier in this chapter using the OCDQ-RM. We now look at Wilson's school climate through another lens, the health of the organization. To simplify our discussion, recall that we often convert the number into

TABLE 5.6 Prototypic Profiles of Contrasting Health Types for Middle Schools

Health Dimension	Healthy School	Unhealthy School
Institutional Integrity	553 (H)	443 (L)
Collegial Leadership	634 (VH)	417 (L)
Principal Influence	623 (VH)	398 (VL)
Resource Support	580 (H)	414 (L)
Teacher Affiliation	613 (VH)	411 (L)
Academic Emphasis	617 (VH)	388 (VL)
Overall health	603 (VH)	412 (L)

NOTE: VH = very high; H = High; VL = very low; L = low.

categories ranging from high to low by using the following conversion table:

Above 550	HIGH
525-550	ABOVE AVERAGE
511-524	SLIGHTLY ABOVE AVERAGE
490-510	AVERAGE
476-489	SLIGHTLY BELOW AVERAGE
450-475	BELOW AVERAGE
Below 450	LOW

Let's revisit the climates of both Wilson and Frost middle schools using the health measure from the OHI-M. Begin with Figure 5.4, which depicts the climate-health profile of Wilson.

Wilson Middle School is a healthy place to work and learn. Wilson is typical of schools in its relationship to the community. Parents place demands on the school, and most teachers don't like them, but the school has reasonable program integrity (average institutional integrity). The principal is a dynamic leader who is respected by teachers as well as superiors. The principal goes to bat for the teachers and is able deliver for them (high principal influence). Teachers at Wilson get whatever resources they need to do the job; all they need do is ask (above average resource support). The principal is one of those gifted administrators who integrates a drive for

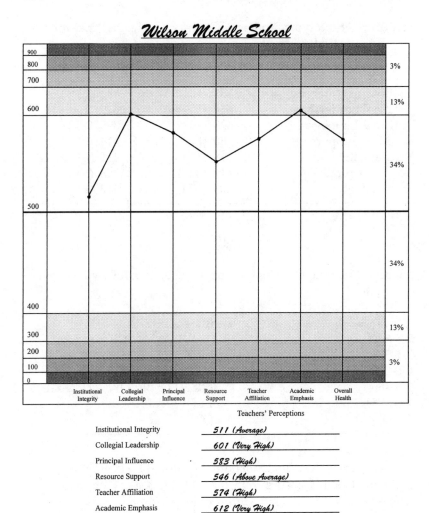

Wilson Middle School

Teachers' Perceptions	
Institutional Integrity	511 (Average)
Collegial Leadership	601 (Very High)
Principal Influence	583 (High)
Resource Support	546 (Above Average)
Teacher Affiliation	574 (High)
Academic Emphasis	612 (Very High)
Overall Health	571 (High)

Figure 5.4. Organizational Health Index for Middle Schools (OHI-M)

the goals of the school with genuine support for teachers (high collegial leadership). Teachers like Wilson. They identify with their school, are proud of their students, and respect each other (high teacher affiliation). Finally, the press for intellectual accomplishment is strong. Teachers set high expectations for their students, and students respond accordingly. The school is pervaded with a sense of purpose in learning (high academic emphasis).

Frost (see Figure 5.5), in contrast, is an unhealthy middle school. Remember that the climate of Frost was also closed. The OHI-M provides additional data and a different perspective on what is wrong with Frost than did the OCDQ-RM. Frost is a school in which outside groups demand change and more control over what goes on in school (low institutional integrity). Instructional materials and supplies are difficult to obtain (low resource support), and the principal has no apparent influence with either teachers (low collegial leadership) or superiors, who ignore him (low principal influence). There is a leadership vacuum. Teachers don't get along with each other and have limited attachment to the school and colleagues (slightly below average teacher affiliation). There are low expectations for student performance, and neither students nor teachers appreciate the hard work it takes to perform academically; teachers have no confidence in the students to achieve (low academic emphasis).

Changing School Climate

You now have the tools to map the climate of your school. Having done so, what's next? It depends on what you find and where you want to go. Problems are discrepancies between what you have and what you want. You have a problem if there is a discrepancy between the profile of climate scores of the principal and those of the teachers. You also have a problem if there is a discrepancy between the actual school scores and what is expected. Ordinarily, you have a problem if the discrepancy puts your school below the scores of the typical healthy school in the normative sample—that is, most educators want to have an average or better school, and the prototypic profiles tell you where your school stands. Remember, a score of less than 500 puts you below the average school. In brief, there are two typical discrepancy problems regarding school climate:

- Discrepancy between the principal's and teachers' perceptions
- Discrepancy between the actual and desired profile of school climate

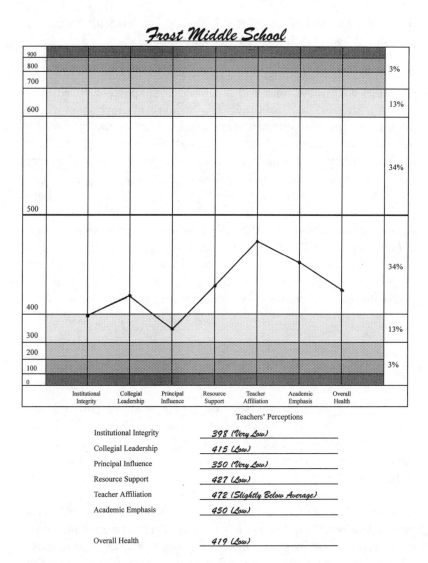

Figure 5.5. Organizational Health Index for Middle Schools (OHI-M)

The challenge to change is formidable, but it is manageable and attainable. We hope to allay your qualms by providing you with an actual example. Before we do that, however, we examine the nature of change and build a model for change—an organizational development model.

Assumptions about Change and Organizations

Before we proceed any further, we think it is useful to make clear some of the basic assumptions on which our analysis for change rests. The following assumptions are critical:

- Change is a property of healthy and open organizations. The principal should see organizations in a constant state of flux. You cannot eliminate change from your school. Change happens, but it can be a random force or a resource harnessed for improvement.
- Change has direction. Change can be progressive, regressive, or random. Schools should neither regress nor drift aimlessly. Progressive change is movement consistent with objectives and eventual solution of problems.
- Organizational learning is possible. Schools can develop their own learning processes to solve their problems. Teachers and principals have high potential to learn how to solve problems together. They both, however, need to see the organization as a whole and be aware of how change affects other parts of the system.
- Schools should be learning organizations, places where "people continually expand their capacity to create the results that they truly desire, where new and expansive patterns of thinking are nurtured, where collective aspiration is set free, and where people are continually learning how to learn" (Senge, 1990, p. 3).
- Healthy and open organizations are not only ends-in-themselves but also the means to learning organizations. Healthy and open schools are characterized by high levels of trust, commitment, and achievement, desirable in themselves. But the process of building school climate naturally transforms the school into a learning organization.

Organizational Development Model

What is a good strategy for insuring healthy, open learning organizations? One useful method for changing school climate is a joint effort on the part of all those concerned, a so-called organizational development approach. Such a perspective addresses both personal and institutional needs, and is a planned effort to make people and eventually organizations more productive (Hanson & Lubin, 1995). This sounds like an approach that might be useful for principals who want to improve the health and openness of their schools. To be successful, this strategy requires that individuals recognize difficulties and take responsibility for their solution. In the case at hand, the objective is to have teachers and the principal recognize that a challenge exists. Identifying the problem has been made manageable because the objective data clearly demonstrate discrepancies between the principal's and the teachers' perceptions of the social interactions in the workplace.

Before proceeding further, we outline the steps in an organizational development approach:

1. *Identify the Problem*—discrepancies in the climate profiles.
2. *Establish a Problem-Solving Team*—usually the teachers in the school. To change climate, teachers must be involved.
3. *The Team Takes On the Problem*—the teachers and principal come to an understanding of the difficulty. Teachers examine the data with the principal and express a willingness to resolve the troubling issues. They must understand the situation and see the need for change.
4. *Diagnose the Problem*—the team diagnoses the causes of the problem.
5. *Develop an Action Plan*—the team develops an action plan by examining alternatives and consequences, and then selecting a course of action.
6. *Implement the Action Plan*—put the plan into action.
7. *Evaluate*—assess the consequences of the plan by collecting new data and evaluating discrepancies.

Sandburg Middle School

Sandburg Middle School distinguishes itself comfortably from other suburban middle schools. It is conspicuous in its consumption of resources. The park-like grounds are as manicured as the rest of the yards in the neighborhood, not surprising given the numbers of professionals living in the community and the scores of gardeners who regularly descend on the town. The children look much like other kids, and the surrounding area is filled with upper-middle-class housing developments. This school is in a wealthy suburban community, in fact, the most affluent in the state. Nelson Poole has been the principal at Sandburg for 6 years. He finished his master's degree and doctorate at a large private university. Dr. Poole, as everyone calls him, has the reputation of being a bright, conscientious, and hardworking principal. He puts in long hours, and few question his commitment to his school. And make no mistake about it: Nelson considers Sandburg his school.

Let's take a look at Sandburg Middle School. First, we examine the climate profiles as described by Dr. Poole. In other words, the following profile is the way Poole described the interactions in his school. He responded to the OHI-M and the OCDQ-RM and followed the directions in scoring the instruments. Poole also had his teachers respond to the same instruments at a faculty meeting. He took pains to get a frank response from the teachers by absenting himself from the meeting and insisting that teachers provide candid responses to the anonymous questionnaires. A comparison of the climate profiles as perceived by the teachers and Poole is found in Figures 5.6 and 5.7.

A quick glance at the profiles signals a problem. Poole describes a much better school than his teachers. Who is right? It doesn't matter. Poole has a problem because the teachers describe his behavior much more negatively than he thinks it is. For instance, he sees his leadership style as open and his teachers perceive it as closed. His teachers describe him as much less supportive, less collegial, less influential, and more directive and restrictive than he does. Poole sees himself as a remarkably supportive and influential leader; his teachers do not. Interestingly, he also describes his teachers' behaviors much more positively than they do. The teachers describe the academic emphasis at Sandburg as average, but Poole sees it as high. The same is true of virtually every health indicator; Poole is a true pollyanna. Poole and his teachers seem to be describing different schools, but they are not. What's happening?

Identifying the problem and solving it call for different strategies. We have used our instruments to identify the problem. As it happens, that's the easy part. What to do is another matter. Poole has to find out why the teachers describe his behavior as more

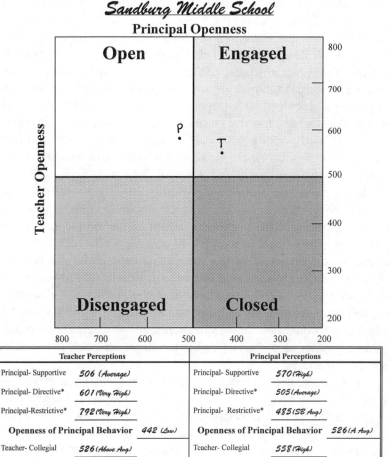

Sandburg Middle School
Principal Openness

Figure 5.6. Organizational Climate Description Questionnaire for Middle Schools (OCDQ-RM)

restrictive, directive, and nonsupportive than he thinks it is. Why does the faculty perceive virtually all interactions in the school as much less positive than Poole does? For example, why is it that the faculty doesn't see the collegial leadership that Poole is trying to model? Why does the faculty describe Dr. Poole's behavior as closed when he sees it as open? It seems clear that Nelson Poole is going to

Sandburg Middle School

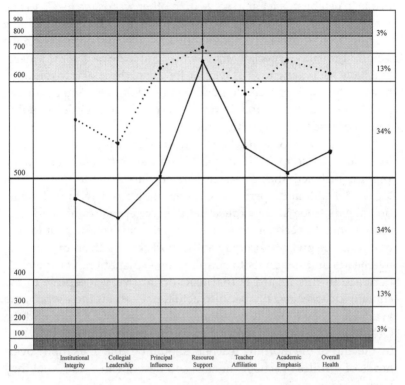

	Teachers' Perceptions	Principal's Perceptions
Institutional Integrity	481 (Slightly Below Avg)	560 (High)
Collegial Leadership	460 (Below Average)	535 (Above Average)
Principal Influence	501 (Average)	650 (Very High)
Resource Support	680 (Very High)	730 (Very High)
Teacher Affiliation	530 (High)	590 (High)
Academic Emphasis	505 (Average)	680 (Very High)
Overall Health	524 (Slightly Above Avg)	624 (Very High)

Figure 5.7. Organizational Health Index for Middle Schools (OHI-M)

have to find a way to communicate with his faculty. This is not a problem he can solve by himself. It is an interaction issue. It may be a question of misperception. But who is misperceiving?

Principal Nelson Poole was startled and dismayed by the school climate data. The teachers clearly see the school as much more negative than he does. This discrepancy in perceptions is a problem that needs to be addressed. Poole has identified the problem. Now, he needs to establish a team to solve it. In other words, he needs to join forces with his teachers and involve them in organizational problem solving. Does this mean that he should involve all the teachers in the school? Probably, especially those who want to be part of the process and have something to say. Over the long run, the goal is to routinely have all teachers participate in decision making and organizational problem solving. Over the short run, the problem is putting together a team of leaders to begin the process.

An easy way to get teachers interested and involved is to use an inservice workshop. Most schools have a day or two throughout the year for such activities. First, teachers need to be made aware of the ideas of health and openness and how they are determined. Some time needs to be spent explicating the conceptual framework and measurement of school climate. In a faculty this small, the information could be given informally at the workshop with accompanying overheads and handouts to simplify the explanation. Our own experience in this regard is that teachers are very receptive to the climate ideas, especially because actual data about their school are available. They typically find the results of the OCDQ-RM and the OHI-M intriguing. And the process can be done in half a day. That is, by the end of the morning teachers should be able to examine overheads of profiles of school climates and describe in detail what they mean.

Next, teachers are ready to look at the profile of their own school as they have described it. The teachers' scores are standardized and presented. The teachers' score for general health is 524 (slightly above average); teacher openness is 538 (above average), but principal openness is 442 (low). From the teachers' vantage point, this is an engaged school: Behavior among the teachers is open and authentic, but interactions between the teachers and the principal are closed. Although the teachers described themselves as relatively open in their dealings with each other, they saw the principal as closed in dealing with them. Why was this? Before answering the question, Poole suggested that they examine his profiles of the school's climate (see Figure 5.6 and 5.7). Now, the discrepancies became even more obvious because the principal saw his behavior as being open whereas the faculty described it as closed (526 vs. 442). Moreover, Poole saw the school as a very healthy place to work and learn and the teachers described the school's health as slightly above average (624 vs. 524). What's happening here? The principal needed to know, and so did the teachers.

This was a time for some straight talk. The principal must ascertain why the teachers saw his behavior as less supportive, more directive, and more restrictive than he did. Poole admitted to the faculty that he was puzzled by the results because he thought his relationship with the faculty was much more positive. Although he was perplexed, he was willing to examine his own values and choices in this public forum. This is not to say he was comfortable in doing so. He wasn't, but he felt constrained to discuss the findings because it was his idea to begin with. At this stage, he had some reservations about the whole project, but he felt he had no choice but to move forward. He tried to convince himself that he needed to have an experimental attitude toward his own behavior and toward his interactions with his teacher colleagues. He had to take some risks to improve the climate of the school, or, at the very least, get his teachers and himself "on the same page." Above all, he wanted a climate of openness and trust in which learning would be continuous. Poole was shaken but determined.

Actually, the problem-solving process was not as dramatic as one might think. There were, after all, only 33 teachers on the faculty and they had not said that the school was bad, only that Poole was too directive and restrictive in his leadership. This was not terrible, but it was bad enough. Poole and the teachers must seek explanations and avoid blaming or scapegoating. Was the problem real? Of course, and the teachers recognized it.

Poole and his teachers had an open conversation about the causes of the discrepancies. Let's listen in:

Poole: I was surprised that the faculty thought vocal parents had easy entrée to the school. I don't think you realize the number of parents I divert at the front office. We don't have real dissatisfaction in the community, but there are people who feel the faculty should have to hear what they want to say about the education of their kids.

Faculty Member: Well, it's true we don't know how much you do, but we do know that too many parents come to see us and complain about things we can't do anything about. It's not a big problem, but it's annoying.

Poole: What do you mean? Give me an example.

Faculty Member: Look, the kids get high marks on the Iowa Tests and yet parents stream in to complain that the scores should be higher. Not everyone can be in the 99th percentile, even here.

Poole: I can't isolate you from the community.

Faculty Member: We know that! But, it's interference nonetheless; and we think you can do better. That's why our scores on institutional integrity differ from yours.

Poole: What do you think I can do? Parents have a right to come into the school.

Faculty Member: Of course they have a right to come in. But, we would like you to head them off and explain about test scores and percentiles.

(Long period of silence)

Poole: Well, well, . . . well, I'll try. We need to talk about this some more. I do understand why we responded to the items on institutional integrity differently. That's useful. But what really surprised me, and I don't understand, was our wholly different views of my leadership. I think of myself as being a lot more supportive and open than you give me credit for.

(Long period of silence)

Faculty Member: Well, we do think of you as supportive, but you lay all sorts of directives and paperwork on us. It's just too much.

Poole: Give me an example.

Faculty Member: To be blunt, you don't give us enough freedom to make the decisions that we need to make. You're an old English teacher, and I am a veteran mathematics teacher. Why do you think you know more about solving quadratic equations than I do?

Poole: I never said I did.

Faculty Member: Well, maybe not, but you leave that kind of impression every time you observe my class. Here's what I mean: I am struggling in class with one of the slower students trying to get him up to speed on work we covered 2 weeks ago. And, you suggest that I should give the students more chance to discover relationships. You claim that I need to be more indirect in my instruction. You just don't understand what's happening in the class.

Poole: I do have other responsibilities, but I am concerned about this problem.

Another Faculty Member: I agree with Bill. You need to treat us more as professionals and less as subordinates. You're a smart guy and you work hard. But you don't see us as equals. You treat us as hired help.

Poole: I don't want to hurt your feelings, but when things go wrong, I am the one accountable. I take the heat, so I want things to run as well as possible.

Faculty Member: You asked for some examples, and you just got two. What are you going to do?

Poole: Well, I'll have to think about this. I appreciate your candor, but it's hard for me not to be defensive. We may have to change some things.

This little exchange should give you a flavor of the kind of conversation that may likely occur. A close analysis of the conversation shows that the principal himself sees a difference in his status and he indirectly communicates it ("I'm the one accountable"). Teachers are seeking more autonomy and some teachers feel the principal doesn't respect their expertise. In other parts of the dialogue, it also became obvious that many teachers felt that occasionally Poole's observations of their performance were critical but neither insightful nor constructive. Moreover, many believed that Poole rarely respected their professional judgments. These were some of the reasons for the discrepancies between Poole's perception of his leadership style and the faculty's perceptions.

What are the causes of these discrepancies? It is at this point that the principal and teachers developed a series of rival explanations for the differences in perceptions. The teachers had to be willing to take some risks in articulating their position without fear of reprisal. The teachers were divided into three groups and each developed an explanation of what was happening. The principal was not part of any group. But rather, Poole also developed a tentative explanation of the data. After an hour or so, the group as a whole reassembled and the four explanations were presented and compared. Now, the principal's chore was to work with the faculty toward some consensus on causes. If no consensus could be reached, then each reasonable explanation should be tested in the weeks and months ahead.

There were four groups, the principal and his assistant and three faculty groups, developing explanations of the discrepancies between the principal and the faculty. After comparing the explanations, the faculty agreed on the following diagnosis:

Parents were going directly to the teachers with their concerns and demands. There was agreement that Poole needed to serve as a buffer between parents and the teachers. Growing out of conversations of the kind that we have just heard, the teachers suggested that Poole would be seen as more collegial and supportive if he would delegate more responsibility and autonomy to them, treat them as full-fledged professionals, and consult more often. A goodly number of teachers also suggested that busywork, such as written, formal lesson plans that go unreviewed, be eliminated. They suggested a committee on paperwork whose charge was to reduce paperwork wherever feasible. For his part, Poole still did not share the explanation of his faculty, but he respected the faculty's judgment and agreed that something needed to be done and he would do it.

Both Poole and the teachers thought that the resource support for teachers was exceptional. Poole saw it as stronger than the teachers but not critically so. Indeed, in the final analysis, everyone felt good about the resource support of the school. The teachers believed that teacher affiliation was lower than Poole observed because, although the teachers were friendly and trusting of each other, at the end of the day they went their separate ways. The teachers agreed that academic emphasis at Sandburg was about average. Poole, however, was unaware that for at least half the teachers, student homework and apathy were problems. Poole was probably misled by the high achievement scores of many students. The students were bright, but not especially committed to academics. Social activities were more important to many students than academic ones.

When it came to the openness of teachers and their relationships, Poole and the teachers more or less agreed that the faculty was open. But there was room for improvement. Although the teachers were committed and engaged in their behavior, they were only above average in collegiality; there was potential for growth here.

Directive and restrictive behavior of the principal were sharp discrepancies between Poole and the faculty. By and large, the teachers believed that his observations of their classroom teaching were perfunctory and harsh. He didn't visit the classrooms often, but when he did, he always had many directives for improvement. The teachers resented the style if not the substance of his comments. The teachers resented the formal sign in and sign out required of all teachers. This was a relatively small school, and everyone knew when others came and went. The teachers resented the extreme formalization in the school—forms for parking, library materials, AV equipment, and grade distribution, repetitive absentee forms, lateness forms, lunch forms, and even a form for the number of minutes spent helping kids after school (which was, after all, a voluntary activity). Teachers found the forms to be restrictive and for the most part unnecessary. Poole saw the forms as a quick way to keep track of things.

How do we develop constructive plans for reducing discrepancies and improving climate? This is the time for the teachers and the principal to work together to forge a realistic plan. There is no one best way to do this, but in the current case the principal and teachers decided to each work on the plan independently and then come back together (much in the same manner as they had framed the causes of the problem) to propose a school improvement plan.

The faculty inservice meeting to discuss and formulate an improvement plan was interesting, to say the least. In response to the analysis of problem causes, the principal thought that he might do the following:

1. Poole at first suggested that the teachers notify his office about instances of parental interference, however the faculty might judge it. Poole would monitor the reports and said if the problem got out of hand, he would step in to buffer the teachers from the parents.

2. Poole was genuinely concerned about the appearance of a heavy-handed, insensitive administration. He proposed to study the amount of paperwork and forms required and reduce them dramatically. He pledged to consult and listen to

his teachers before acting. He thought highly of his teachers and conceded that they should have more independence in making professional judgments. In fact, he proposed that a leadership cabinet be formed, composed of all the team leaders to share in decision making in the school. Finally, he proposed that the team leaders and the teachers should develop a program of peer supervision. In essence, Poole proposed a delegation of authority and responsibility to his teachers. Although he thought lesson plans were necessary to insure a coherent curriculum, he was willing to delegate this responsibility to teachers and team leaders.

3. The discrepancy between Poole's perception of teacher collegiality and the teachers' judgment probably erred on the side of optimism and seemed of no great consequence. Poole may have overgeneralized about the teachers, but he was determined to involve his teachers in collaborative efforts in which they enjoyed working with each other professionally. To that end, he proposed that the next inservice day be devoted to developing strategies for joint curriculum development across interdisciplinary teams.

4. Poole promised that he would make himself more readily available to the faculty. He also pledged that in the future, his criticism would be constructive and helpful. He concluded by reaffirming confidence and admiration for his faculty and pointed out the one area in which there was virtual agreement was the commitment of the teachers to the students.

5. Finally, Poole was concerned about the academic seriousness of the school. This was a good school in a community that supported education. He was shocked to find his teachers did not share his perception of the academic climate of Sandburg Middle School. He vowed to address the issue on a number of fronts. First, a series of meetings with his faculty was necessary to discover the origin of the faculty's assessment of the mediocre academic press at Sandburg.

The faculty for its part came in with the following set of recommendations:

1. The teachers proposed that Poole become actively involved as a liaison between teachers and parents. In particular, they

recommended that the team leaders together with Poole and the executive committee of the PTA meet regularly to address and mollify parental concerns.

2. The teachers proposed a system of peer coaching to improve the teaching-learning process. They asked that they be given more input into future inservice meetings.

3. Because Sandburg was a such a small school, the faculty proposed that the principal consult with them informally about important school issues. They didn't want more meetings, just more influence and information.

4. The teachers recommended that a committee of teachers be appointed to streamline the bureaucratic procedures of the school—no more forms.

5. The teachers recommended that a schoolwide policy be established on homework and tutorials. The honor society would be approached and asked to do volunteer tutoring a few afternoons a week.

After the suggestions and recommendations were enumerated and discussed, Poole and the faculty were concerned about the number of different issues that surfaced and the time needed to confront them. Poole, for his part, admitted that he was unrealistically optimistic and the whole exercise provided him with a reality check. The teachers, on the other hand, were a little afraid that if they tried to do too much, nothing would be accomplished. They needed a reasonable plan that was realistic and attainable. There was, however, an inherent dilemma in their suggestions: They wanted greater involvement and more interaction but fewer meetings and less administrative work. They agreed to be idealistic and yet pragmatic. The following aspects were key elements of their eventual plan.

1. Four teachers volunteered to work with the principal to find ways to reduce paperwork, unnecessary meetings, and administrative routine.

2. Poole and the teachers agreed that team leaders, the executive committee of the PTA, and Poole would meet regularly to address community concerns.

3. Formal lesson plans were eliminated as a requirement, but teachers agreed to have an outline of the class activities for the

week. They also agreed that when one was absent, they would help each other by aiding the substitute and by keeping in touch with the absent teacher. Team leaders were given the responsibility of coordinating this process.

4. Poole agreed with the teachers that a system of peer coaching should be initiated. Teachers agreed to combine classes on occasion so that they could serve as teaching models and coaches for each other.

5. The faculty and Poole agreed that a leadership cabinet composed of team leaders and elected teachers should be formed to share in the governance of the school. Poole agreed to consult with the faculty cabinet concerning all matters in which teachers had a personal stake and professional knowledge. Poole suggested and the teachers agreed that the faculty would have complete independence in planning the programs for the three inservice days of professional development next year.

Clearly, this plan is not a set of step-by-step procedures to be accomplished in a rigid way. To the contrary, the plan is a set of accepted guidelines and commitments.

How will this plan be implemented? Lesson plans will be eliminated as a formal requirement immediately (Item 3). The paperwork committee (Item 1), as the teachers called it, agreed to meet in the next several weeks and would have recommendations back to the faculty and principal in 2 months. Another committee of teachers would be formed to plan the specifics for the peer-coaching experiment (Item 4). The principal decided to set aside a portion of each regular faculty meeting for faculty governance (Item 5). The teachers and principal realized that their plan required increased effort. It is ironic that a major goal of the plan was to reduce unnecessary busywork, yet the cost of involvement, professional control, and autonomy was more work to do. The faculty is committed to the plan even though they know it will be more work, but meaningful work.

How successful would this plan be? That is an empirical question. In 6 months, two activities would occur to assess its effectiveness. First, the OCDQ-RM and OHI-M would be administered and scored, and then the principal and faculty would revisit the climate and changes at Sandburg.

Just to keep things in perspective, let us review what has happened in the inservice at Sandburg. The morning of the first day was spent explaining, discussing, and interpreting the climate frameworks, their measures, and the school profiles. In the afternoon, the teachers were confronted with the openness and health profiles of Sandburg. After some discussion of those profiles and agreement on what they meant, the principal introduced his perception of the school profile, which diverged dramatically from that of the faculty. The discrepancies led to a frank and open discussion between the principal and teachers culminating in the formation of three teacher groups to develop tentative explanations about the causes of the discrepancies in perceptions. After working in small groups for an hour or so, the teachers reconvened and shared their explanations, coming to a rough consensus about the causes of the discrepancy. The next day was spent formulating a plan to reduce the discrepancies and improve the health and openness of the school. These two inservice days should be thought of as a beginning of a continuous program of improvement and problem solving. Even if these educators are successful in developing the school climate they all desire, periodic monitoring of climate is a wise course. We hope that through this process two things occur: first, the climate of the school is improved, and second, group problem solving and organizational learning become natural elements of school life.

Conclusion

This chapter is a brief description of the Organizational Climate Description Questionnaire (OCDQ-RM) and Organizational Health Inventory for middle schools (OHI-M). We suggest how to administer and use these tools. Copy the instruments, administer them, and score them. For clean copies of the OCDQ-RM and the OHI-M, see the appendix. There is no copyright restriction; feel free to make as many copies as you wish. Then, determine your school's climate profile and evaluate it. Do you want to improve or change the climate? Before you engage in a school improvement plan, we suggest, if you haven't already done so, that you assess the organizational climate using both climate instruments. With both openness and health profiles in hand and knowledge of your own school, you are in a better position to plan change.

With this book, you have the tools for change. The data you gather from these measures can make a significant impact, if commitment to school improvement is combined with a leader who is prepared to develop an inclusive process of change. With improved climate you can look forward to such other related outcomes as increased faculty commitment, faculty trust, and eventually increased student achievement. It won't be easy. Constructive change rarely is; it has its costs. We believe, however, the results of such analyses and improvement plans will produce a more productive and positive school environment for students, teachers, administrators, and parents—in short, quality middle schools.

Notes

1. This chapter draws heavily from Hoy and Tarter (1997a, 1997b). I am particularly indebted to my friend and colleague, John Tarter, who worked with me in developing the ideas in this chapter.

2. Computer scoring programs for both the OCDQ-RM and the OHI-M are available from Arlington Writers, 2548 Onandaga Drive, Columbus, Ohio 43221. The programs, which run on Windows 95, will score each subtest, standardize school scores, and provide indexes of openness and health. Information and cost of the scoring program are found in the appendix; further information can be obtained from Arlington Writers (fax 614 488-5075).

3. The real names of the schools and principals in this book have been changed.

Appendix

OCDQ-RM

Directions: The following are statements about your school. Please indicate the extent to which each statement characterizes your school by circling the appropriate response.

RO = Rarely Occurs   SO = Sometimes Occurs   O = Often Occurs
VFO = Very Frequently Occurs

1. The principal compliments teachers.	RO SO O VFO
2. Teachers have parties for each other.	RO SO O VFO
3. Teachers are burdened with busywork.	RO SO O VFO
4. Routine duties interfere with the job of teaching.	RO SO O VFO
5. Teachers "go the extra mile" with their students.	RO SO O VFO
6. Teachers are committed to helping their students.	RO SO O VFO
7. Teachers help students on their own time.	RO SO O VFO
8. Teachers interrupt other teachers who are talking in staff meetings.	RO SO O VFO
9. The principal rules with an iron fist.	RO SO O VFO
10. The principal encourages teacher autonomy.	RO SO O VFO
11. The principal goes out of his or her way to help teachers.	RO SO O VFO
12. The principal is available after school to help teachers when assistance is needed.	RO SO O VFO
13. Teachers invite other faculty members to visit them at home.	RO SO O VFO
14. Teachers socialize with each other on a regular basis.	RO SO O VFO
15. The principal uses constructive criticism.	RO SO O VFO
16. Teachers who have personal problems receive support from other staff members.	RO SO O VFO
17. Teachers stay after school to tutor students who need help.	RO SO O VFO
18. Teachers accept additional duties if students will benefit.	RO SO O VFO
19. The principal looks out for the personal welfare of the faculty.	RO SO O VFO
20. The principal supervises teachers closely.	RO SO O VFO
21. Teachers leave school immediately after school is over.	RO SO O VFO

22. Most of the teachers here accept the faults of their colleagues. RO SO O VFO
23. Teachers exert group pressure on nonconforming faculty members. RO SO O VFO
24. The principal listens to and accepts teachers' suggestions. RO SO O VFO
25. Teachers have fun socializing together during school time. RO SO O VFO
26. Teachers ramble when they talk at faculty meetings. RO SO O VFO
27. Teachers are rude to other staff members. RO SO O VFO
28. Teachers make "wise cracks" to each other during meetings. RO SO O VFO
29. Teachers mock teachers who are different. RO SO O VFO
30. Teachers don't listen to other teachers. RO SO O VFO
31. Teachers like to hear gossip about other staff members. RO SO O VFO
32. The principal treats teachers as equals. RO SO O VFO
33. The principal corrects teachers' mistakes. RO SO O VFO
34. Teachers provide strong social support for colleagues. RO SO O VFO
35. Teachers respect the professional competence of their colleagues. RO SO O VFO
36. The principal goes out of his or her way to show appreciation to teachers. RO SO O VFO
37. The principal keeps a close check on sign-in times. RO SO O VFO
38. The principal monitors everything teachers do. RO SO O VFO
39. Administrative paperwork is burdensome at this school. RO SO O VFO
40. Teachers help and support each other. RO SO O VFO
41. The principal closely checks teacher activities. RO SO O VFO
42. Assigned nonteaching duties are excessive. RO SO O VFO
43. The interactions between team/unit members are cooperative. RO SO O VFO
44. The principal accepts and implements ideas suggested by faculty members. RO SO O VFO
45. Members of teams/units consider other members to be their friends. RO SO O VFO
46. Extra help is available to students who need help. RO SO O VFO
47. Teachers volunteer to sponsor after-school activities. RO SO O VFO
48. Teachers spend time after school with students who have individual problems. RO SO O VFO
49. The principal sets an example by working hard himself or herself. RO SO O VFO
50. Teachers are polite to one another. RO SO O VFO

Dimensions of Organizational Climate (OCDQ-RM)

Principal's Behavior

Supportive behavior is directed toward both the social needs and task achievement of faculty. The principal is helpful, is genuinely concerned with teachers, and attempts to motivate by using constructive criticism and by setting an example through hard work.

Directive behavior is rigid, domineering behavior. The principal maintains close and constant monitoring over virtually all aspects of teacher behavior in the school.

Restrictive behavior is behavior that hinders rather than facilitates teacher work. The principal burdens teachers with paperwork, committee requirements, and other demands that interfere with their teaching responsibilities.

Teachers' Behavior

Collegial behavior supports open and professional interactions among teachers. Teachers like, respect, and help one another both professionally and personally.

Committed behavior is directed toward helping students to develop both socially and intellectually. Teachers work extra hard to insure student success in school.

Disengaged behavior signifies a lack of meaning and focus to professional activities. Teachers are simply putting in their time; in fact, they are critical and unaccepting of their colleagues.

OCDQ-RM Profile
Organizational Climate Description Questionnaire for Middle Schools

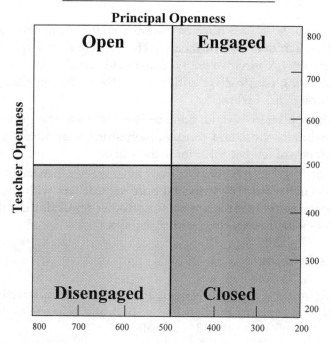

Teacher Perceptions		Principal Perceptions	
Principal- Supportive		Principal- Supportive	
Principal- Directive*		Principal- Directive*	
Principal- Restrictive*		Principal- Restrictive*	
Openness of Principal Behavior		**Openness of Principal Behavior**	
Teacher- Collegial		Teacher- Collegial	
Teacher- Committed		Teacher- Committed	
Teacher- Disengaged*		Teacher- Disengaged*	
Openness of Teacher Behavior		**Openness of Teacher Behavior**	
Total Openness		**Total Openness**	

*Reverse Scored in Composites

OHI-M

Directions: The following are statements about your school. Please indicate the extent to which each statement characterizes your school by circling the appropriate response.

RO = Rarely Occurs   SO = Sometimes Occurs   O = Often Occurs
VFO = Very Frequently Occurs

1. The principal explores all sides of topics and admits that other options exist.   RO SO O   VFO
2. Students make provisions to acquire extra help from teachers.   RO SO O   VFO
3. The principal gets what he or she asks for from superiors.   RO SO O   VFO
4. The principal discusses classroom issues with teachers.   RO SO O   VFO
5. The principal accepts questions without appearing to snub or quash the teacher.   RO SO O   VFO
6. Extra materials are available if requested.   RO SO O   VFO
7. Students neglect to complete homework.   RO SO O   VFO
8. The school is vulnerable to outside pressures.   RO SO O   VFO
9. The principal is able to influence the actions of his or her superiors.   RO SO O   VFO
10. The principal treats all faculty members as his or her equal.   RO SO O   VFO
11. Teachers are provided with adequate materials for their classrooms.   RO SO O   VFO
12. Teachers in this school like each other.   RO SO O   VFO
13. Community demands are accepted even when they are not consistent with the educational program.   RO SO O   VFO
14. The principal lets faculty know what is expected of them.   RO SO O   VFO
15. Teachers receive necessary classroom supplies.   RO SO O   VFO
16. Students respect others who get good grades.   RO SO O   VFO
17. Good grades are important to the students of this school.   RO SO O   VFO
18. Teachers feel pressure from the community.   RO SO O   VFO
19. The principal's recommendations are given serious consideration by his or her superiors.   RO SO O   VFO
20. Supplementary materials are available for classroom use.   RO SO O   VFO
21. Teachers exhibit friendliness to each other.   RO SO O   VFO
22. Students seek extra work so they can get good grades.   RO SO O   VFO

23. Select citizen groups are influential with the
    board.   RO SO O VFO
24. The principal looks out for the personal
    welfare of faculty members.   RO SO O VFO
25. The school is open to the whims of the public.   RO SO O VFO
26. A few vocal parents can change school policy.   RO SO O VFO
27. Students try hard to improve on previous
    work.   RO SO O VFO
28. Teachers accomplish their jobs with
    enthusiasm.   RO SO O VFO
29. The learning environment is orderly and serious. RO   SO O VFO
30. The principal is friendly and approachable.   RO SO O VFO
31. Teachers show commitment to their students.   RO SO O VFO
32. Teachers are indifferent to each other.   RO SO O VFO
33. Teachers are protected from unreasonable
    community and parental demands.   RO SO O VFO
34. The principal is able to work well with the
    superintendent.   RO SO O VFO
35. The principal is willing to make changes.   RO SO O VFO
36. Teachers have access to needed instructional
    materials.   RO SO O VFO
37. Teachers in this school are cool and aloof to
    each other.   RO SO O VFO
38. Teachers in this school believe that their
    students have the ability to achieve
    academically.   RO SO O VFO
39. The principal is understanding when personal
    concerns cause teachers to arrive late or leave
    early.   RO SO O VFO
40. Our school gets its fair share of resources from
    the district.   RO SO O VFO
41. The principal is rebuffed by the
    superintendent.   RO SO O VFO
42. Teachers volunteer to help each other.   RO SO O VFO
43. The principal is effective in securing the
    superintendent's approval for new programs
    or activities.   RO SO O VFO
44. Academically oriented students in this school
    are ridiculed by their peers.   RO SO O VFO
45. Teachers do favors for each other.   RO SO O VFO

Dimensions of Organizational Health
of Middle Schools (OHI-M)

Institutional Level

Institutional integrity describes a school that has integrity in its educational program. The school is not vulnerable to narrow, vested interests of community groups; indeed, teachers are protected from unreasonable community and parental demands. The school is able to cope successfully with destructive outside forces.

Administrative Level

Collegial leadership is principal behavior that is friendly, supportive, open, and guided by norms of equality. But, at the same time, the principal sets the tone for high performance by letting people know what is expected of them.

Resource support refers primarily to classroom supplies and instructional materials. They are readily available; indeed, extra materials are supplied if requested.

Principal influence is the principal's ability to influence the actions of superiors. Influential principals are persuasive with superiors, get additional consideration, and proceed relatively unimpeded by the hierarchy.

Teacher Level

Teacher affiliation is a sense of friendliness and strong affiliation with the school. Teachers feel good about each other, their job, and their students. They are committed to both their students and their colleagues and accomplish their jobs with enthusiasm.

Academic emphasis is the extent to which the school is driven by a quest for academic excellence. High but achievable academic goals are set for students; the learning environment is orderly and serious; teachers believe in their students' ability to achieve; and students work hard and respect those who do well academically.

OHI-M Profile
Organizational Health Index for Middle Schools

900								
800								3%
700								
600								13%
								34%
500								
								34%
400								
300								13%
200								
100								3%
0								
	Institutional Integrity	Collegial Leadership	Principal Influence	Resource Support	Teacher Affiliation	Academic Emphasis	Overall Health	

	Teachers' Perceptions	Principal's Perceptions
Institutional Integrity	_____	_____
Collegial Leadership	_____	_____
Principal Influence	_____	_____
Resource Support	_____	_____
Teacher Affiliation	_____	_____
Academic Emphasis	_____	_____
Overall Health	_____	_____

Dear School Administrator:

We'd be interested in your results. If you'd be willing to share them with us, it will help us learn more about the climate of schools. All results are confidential — in fact, we have no place on the form for the name of the school or principal.

To send this form to us just fold it, tape it shut, and stamp it; or else place it in an envelope and send it to the address below.

Place
Postage
Stamp
Here

Dr. Wayne Hoy
The Ohio State University
29 W. Woodruff Ave.
Columbus, OH 43210-1177

All data pertains to the school. Approximate population and enrollment figures are adequate.

Country & Zip Code	State and Region of the Country
Population of the city or town where the school is located	Environment ____ Urban ____ Suburban ____ Rural
Number of students in the district	Grade levels in the school district ____ – ____
Number of students in your school	Percent of students on free and reduced lunch ____
Type and grade levels of your school ____ Middle School ____ Junior High ____ Secondary	Demographics ____% African-American ____% Asian-American ____% European-American ____% Latino-American ____% Other

Scores on the OHI-M			
Raw Scores		Standardized Scores	
Overall Health		Overall Health	
Institutional Integrity		Institutional Integrity	
Collegial Leadership		Collegial Leadership	
Principal Influence		Principal Influence	
Resource Support		Resource Support	
Teacher Affiliation		Teacher Affiliation	
Academic Emphasis		Academic Emphasis	

Scores on the OCDQ-RM			
Raw Scores		Standardized Scores	
Supportive		Supportive	
Directive		Directive	
Restrictive		Restrictive	
Principal Openness		**Principal Openness**	
Collegial		Collegial	
Committed		Committed	
Disengaged		Disengaged	
Teacher Openness		**Teacher Openness**	

Computer Scoring Program
Order Form

Name	
Institution	
Address	
City	
State	
Zip Code	
Telephone	

	Price	Quantity	Cost
Elementary School Package (OCDQ-RE & OHI-E)	$200.00		
Middle School Package (OCDQ-RM & OHI-M)	$200.00		
Secondary School Package (OCDQ-RS & OHI-S)	$200.00		
All Three Packages	$500.00		
Postage & Handling	$3.00		$3.00
Total			

Order by Mail or by FAX
Arlington Writers Ltd. 2548 Onandaga Drive Columbus, OH 43221
FAX 614-488-5075
Pay by Check or attach a Purchase Order

REFERENCES

Alexander, W. M., & George, P. S. (1981). *The exemplary middle school*. New York: Holt, Rinehart & Winston.

Alluto, J. A., & Belasco, J. A. (1972). A typology of participation in organizational decision making. *Administrative Science Quarterly, 17*, 117-125.

American Association of School Administrators. (1991). *An introduction to total quality management: A collection of articles on the concepts of total quality management and W. Edwards Deming*. Arlington, VA: Author.

Anderson, C. S. (1982). The search for school climate: A review of the research. *Review of Educational Research, 52*, 368-420.

Anderson, G. J., & Walberg, H. J. (1974). Learning environments. In H. J. Walberg (Ed.), *Evaluating educational performance* (pp. 241-268). San Francisco, CA: Jossey-Bass.

Andrews, J. H. M. (1965). School organizational climate: Some validity studies. *Canadian Education and Research Digest, 5*, 317-334.

Appleberry, J. B., & Hoy, W. K. (1969). The pupil control ideology of professional personnel in open and closed elementary schools. *Educational Administration Quarterly, 5*, 74-85.

Argyris, C. (1964). *Integrating the individual and the organization*. New York: John Wiley.

Armor, D., Corny-Oseguera, P., Cox, M., King, N., McDonnell, L., Pascal, A., Pauly, E., & Zellman, G. (1976). *Analysis of the school preferred reading program in selected Los Angeles minority schools*. Santa Monica, CA: RAND.

Ash, P. A. (1992). *Organizational health and teachers' concerns about an innovation*. Unpublished doctoral dissertation, Rutgers University, New Brunswick, NJ.

Ashforth, S. J. (1985). Climate formations: Issues and extensions. *Academy of Management Review, 25,* 837-847.

Ashton, P. T., & Webb, R. B. (1986). *Making a difference: Teachers' sense of efficacy and student achievement*. New York: Longman.

Bacharach, S. B., Bauer, S., & Conely, S. (1986). Organizational analysis of stress: The case of elementary and secondary schools. *Work and Occupations, 13,* 7-32.

Barnard, C. L. (1938). *Functions of the executive*. Cambridge, MA: Harvard University Press.

Barnes, K. M. (1994). *The organizational health of middle schools, trust, and decision participation*. Unpublished doctoral dissertation, Rutgers University, New Brunswick, NJ.

Barth, R. (1990). *Improving schools from within*. San Francisco, CA: Jossey-Bass.

Bennis, W. (1989). *On becoming a leader*. Reading, MA: Addison-Wesley.

Blau, P. M., & Scott, W. R. (1961). *Formal organizations*. San Francisco: Chandler.

Bonstingl, J. J. (1994). The quality revolution in education. *Educational Leadership, 50,* 4-9.

Borton, W. W. (1991, April). *Empowering teachers and students in a restructuring school: A teacher efficacy interactional model and the effect on reading outcomes*. Paper presented at the annual meeting of the American Educational Research Association, Chicago.

Bossert, S. T. (1988). School effects. In N. J. Boyan (Ed.), *Handbook of research on educational administration* (pp. 341-352). New York: Longman.

Brookover, W. B., Schweitzer, J. H., Schneider, J. M., Beady, C. H., Flood, P. K., & Wisenbaker, J. M. (1979). Elementary school social climate and school achievement. *American Educational Research Journal, 15,* 301-318.

Brown, R. J. (1965). *Identifying and classifying organizational climates in Twin City area elementary schools*. Unpublished doctoral dissertation, University of Minnesota, Minneapolis.

Brumbaugh, R. B. (1971). Authenticity and theories of administrative behavior. *Administrative Science Quarterly, 16,* 108-112.

Bryk, A., Lee, V., & Holland, P. (1993). *Catholic schools and the common good*. Cambridge, MA: Harvard University Press.

Cameron, K., & Whetten, D. A. (1983). *Organizational effectiveness: A comparison of multiple models*. New York: Academic Press.

Cameron, K., & Whetten, D. A. (1995). Organizational effectiveness and quality: The second generation. *Higher Education: Handbook of Theory and Research, 11,* 265-306.

Capper, C. A., & Jamison, M. T. (1993). Let the buyer beware: Total quality management and educational research and practice. *Educational Researcher, 22,* 25-30.

Carnegie Task Force on Young Adolescents. (1989). *Turning points: Preparing American youth for the 21st century.* Washington, DC: Carnegie Council on Adolescent Development.

Carver, F., & Sergiovanni, T. (1969). Notes on the OCDQ. *Journal of Educational Administration, 7,* 71-81.

Cawelti, G. (1988). Middle schools a better match with early adolescent needs, ASCD survey finds. *ASCD Curriculum Update.* (Available from Association for Supervision and Curriculum Development, 125 North West Street, Alexandria, VA)

Childers, J. H., & Fairman, M. (1985). Organizational health: School counselor as facilitator. *Planning and Changing, 16,* 161-166.

Clark, E., & Fairman, M. (1983). Organizational health: A significant force in planned change. *NASSP Bulletin, 67,* 108-113.

Conway, J. (1976). Test of linearity between teachers' participation in decision making and their perceptions of their schools as organizations. *Administrative Science Quarterly, 21,* 130-139.

Corwin, R. G., & Borman, K. M. (1988). School as workplace: Structural constraints on administration. In N. Boyan (Ed.), *Handbook of research on educational administration* (pp. 209-237). New York: Longman.

Cronbach, L. J. (1989). Construct validation after 30 years. In R. E. Linn (Ed.), *Intelligence: Measurement, theory and public policy* (pp. 147-171). Urbana: University of Illinois.

Cuban, L. (1992). What happens to reforms that last? The case of the junior high school. *American Educational Research Journal, 29,* 227-252.

Deal, T., & Kennedy, A. (1982). *Corporate cultures.* Reading, MA: Addison-Wesley.

Deming, W. E. (1983). *Quality, productivity, and competitive advantage.* Cambridge: Massachusetts Institute of Technology, Center for Advanced Engineering.

Deming, W. E. (1986). *Out of crisis.* Cambridge: Massachusetts Institute of Technology, Center for Advanced Engineering.

Deming, W. E. (1993). *The new economics for economics, government, education.* Cambridge: Massachusetts Institute of Technology, Center for Advanced Engineering.

Denison, D. R. (1996). What is the difference between organizational culture and organizational climate? A native's point of view on a decade of paradigm wars. *Academy of Management Review, 21,* 619-654.

Edmonds, R. R. (1979). Effective schools for the urban poor. *Educational Leadership, 37,* 15-24.

Finneran, R. J. (1990). *The effects of social climate, minimal competency testing (HSPT), and teacher efficacy on teacher stress.* Unpublished doctoral dissertation, Rutgers University, New Brunswick, NJ.

Firestone, W. A., & Wilson, B. L. (1985). Using bureaucratic and cultural linkages to improve instruction: The principal's contribution. *Educational Administration Quarterly, 20,* 7-13.

Forehand, G. A., & Gilmer, B. (1964). Environmental variation in studies of organizational behavior. *Psychological Bulletin, 62,* 361-381.

Geertz, C. (1973). *The interpretation of cultures.* New York: Basic Books.

Gellerman, S. (1959). The company personality. *Management Review, 48,* 69-76.

Getzels, J. W., Lipham, J. M., & Campbell, R. F. (1968). *Educational administration as a social process: Theory, research, and practice.* New York: Harper & Row.

Gilmer, B. (1966). *Industrial psychology* (2nd ed.). New York: McGraw-Hill.

Glaub, J. (1990). Made in Japan. *Illinois School Board Journal, 58,* 5-7.

Golembiewski, T. T., & McConkie, M. (1975). The centrality of interpersonal trust in group processes. In C. L. Cooper (Ed.), *Theories of group process* (pp. 131-185). New York: McGraw-Hill.

Goodenough, W. (1971). *Culture, language, and society.* Reading, MA: Addison-Wesley.

Gronlund, N. E. (1993). *How to make achievement tests and assessments.* Boston: Allyn & Bacon.

Guskey, T. (1988). Teacher efficacy, self-concept, and attitudes toward the implementation of instructional innovation. *Teaching and Teacher Education, 4,* 63-69.

Halpin, A. W. (1966). *Theory and research in administration.* New York: Macmillan.

Halpin, A. W., & Croft, D. (1962, August). *The organizational climate of schools* (Research Project, Contract No. SAE 543-8639). Washington, DC: U.S. Office of Education.

Halpin, A. W., & Croft, D. B. (1963). *The organizational climate of schools.* Chicago: University of Chicago, Midwest Administration Center.

Hannum, J. W. (1994). *The organizational climate of middle schools, teacher efficacy, and student achievement.* Unpublished doctoral dissertation, Rutgers University, New Brunswick, NJ.

Hannum, J., Hoy, W. K., & Sabo, D. (1996, April). *Organizational health and student achievement in middle schools.* Paper presented at the annual meeting of the American Educational Research Association, New York.

Hanson, P. G., & Lubin, B. (1995). *Answers to questions most frequently asked about organization development.* Thousand Oaks, CA: Sage.

Hayes, A. W. (1973). *A reappraisal of the Halpin-Croft model of the organizational climate of schools.* Paper presented at the American Educational Research Association, New Orleans.

Henderson, J. E., & Hoy, W. K. (1982). Leader authenticity: The development and test of an operational measure. *Educational and Psychological Research, 3,* 63-75.

Hoffman, J. D. (1993). *The organizational climate of middle schools and dimensions of authenticity and trust.* Unpublished doctoral dissertation, Rutgers University, New Brunswick, NJ.

Hoffman, J. D., Sabo, D., Bliss, J. R., & Hoy, W. K. (1994). Building a culture of trust. *Journal of School Leadership, 3,* 484-501.

Homans, G. C. (1950). *The human group.* New York: Harcourt Brace.

Hoy, W. K. (1972). Dimensions of student alienation and characteristics of public high schools. *Interchange, 3,* 36-52.

Hoy, W. K. (1990). Organizational climate and culture: A conceptual analysis of the school workplace. *Journal of Educational and Psychological Consultation, 1,* 149-168.

Hoy, W. K., & Barnes, K. (1997, April). *The organizational health of middle schools: The concept and its measure.* Paper presented at the annual meeting of the American Educational Research Association, Chicago.

Hoy, W. K., & Clover, S. I. R. (1986). Elementary school climate: A revision of the OCDQ. *Educational Administration Quarterly, 22,* 93-110.

Hoy, W. K., & Feldman, J. A. (1987). Organizational health: The concept and its measure. *Journal of Research and Development in Education, 20,* 30-38.

Hoy, W. K., & Ferguson, J. (1985). A theoretical framework and exploration of organizational effectiveness. *Educational Administration Quarterly, 21,* 117-134.

Hoy, W. K., & Forsyth, P. B. (1986). *Effective supervision: Theory into practice.* New York: Random House.

Hoy, W. K., & Hannum, J. (1997). Middle school climate: An empirical assessment of organizational health and student achievement. *Educational Administration Quarterly, 33,* 290-311.

Hoy, W. K., & Henderson, J. E. (1983). Principal authenticity, school climate, and pupil-control orientation. *Alberta Journal of Educational Research, 2,* 123-130.

Hoy, W. K., Hoffman, J., Sabo, D., & Bliss, J. R. (1996). The organizational climate of middle schools: The development and test of the OCDQ-RM. *Journal of Educational Administration, 34,* 41-59.

Hoy, W. K., & Kupersmith, W. J. (1985). The meaning and measure of faculty trust. *Educational and Psychological Research, 5,* 1-10.

Hoy, W. K., & Miskel, C. G. (1987). *Educational administration: Theory, research, and practice* (3rd ed.). New York: Random House.

Hoy, W. K., & Miskel, C. G. (1991). *Educational administration: Theory, research, and practice* (4th ed.). New York: McGraw-Hill.

Hoy, W. K., & Miskel, C. G. (1996). *Educational administration: Theory, research, and practice (5th ed).* New York: McGraw-Hill.

Hoy, W. K., & Tarter, C. J. (1997a). *The road to open and healthy schools: A handbook for change* (middle and secondary school ed.). Thousands Oaks, CA: Corwin.

Hoy, W. K., & Tarter, C. J. (1997b). *The road to open and healthy schools: A handbook for change* (elementary and middle school ed.). Thousands Oaks, CA: Corwin.

Hoy, W. K., Tarter, C. J., & Kottkamp, R. B. (1991). *Open schools/healthy schools: Measuring organizational climate.* Newbury Park, CA: Sage.

Hoy, W. K., Tarter, C. J., & Witkoskie, L. (1992). Faculty trust in colleagues: Linking the principal with school effectiveness. *Journal of Research and Development in Education, 26*(1), 40-47.

Hoy, W. K., & Woolfolk, A. E. (1990). Socialization of student teachers. *American Educational Research Journal, 27,* 279-300.

Johnson, S. M. (1990). *Teachers at work: Achieving success in our schools.* New York: Basic Books.

Kilmann, R. H., Saxton, M. J., Serpa, R., & Associates (1985). *Gaining control of the corporate culture.* San Francisco: Jossey-Bass.

Kimpston, R. D., & Sonnabend, L. C. (1975). Public schools: The inter-relationships between organizational health and innovativeness and between organizational health and staff characteristics. *Urban Education, 10,* 27-48.

Kottkamp, R. B., Mulhern, J. A., & Hoy, W. K. (1987). Secondary school climate: A revision of the OCDQ. *Educational Administration Quarterly, 23,* 31-48.

Koys, D., & Decotiis, T. (1991). Inductive measures of psychological climate. *Human Relations, 44,* 265-285.

Leonard, J. F. (1991). Applying Deming's principles to our schools. *South Carolina Business, 11,* 82-87.

Likert, R. (1961). *New patterns of management.* New York: McGraw-Hill.

Likert, R. (1967). *The human organization: Its management and value.* New York: McGraw-Hill.

Lipham, J. M. (1974). Improving the decision-making skills of the principal. In J. A. Culbertson, C. Henson, & R. Morrison (Eds.), *Performance objectives for school principals* (pp. 146-189). Berkeley, CA: McCutchan.

Little, J. W. (1987). Teachers as colleagues. In V. Richardson-Koehler (Ed.), *Educator's handbook: A research perspective* (pp. 491-518). White Plains, NY: Longman.

Litwin, G. H., & Stringer, R. A., Jr. (1968). *Motivation and organizational climate.* Boston: Harvard Business School, Division of Research.

Lorsch, J. W. (1985). Strategic myopia: Culture as an invisible barrier to change. In R. H. Kilmann, M. J. Saxton, R. Serpa, & Associates (Eds.), *Gaining control of the corporate culture* (pp. 84-102). San Francisco: Jossey-Bass.

Malinowski, B. (1961). *Argonauts of the western Pacific.* London: Routledge & Kegan Paul.

Martin, J. (1985). Can organizational culture be managed? In P. J. Frost, L. F. Moore, M. R. Louis, C. C. Lundberg, & J. Martin (Eds.), *Organizational culture* (pp. 95-98). Beverly Hills, CA: Sage.

Mayo, E. (1945). *The social problems of industrial civilization.* Boston: Harvard University, Graduate School of Business Administration.

McDill, E. L., Meyers, E. D., & Rigby, L. C. (1967). Institutional effects on the academic behavior of high school students. *Sociology of Education, 40,* 181-189.

McGregor, D. (1960). *The human side of enterprise.* New York: McGraw-Hill.

Meany, D. P. (1991). Quest for quality. *California Technology Project Quarterly, 2,* 8-15.

Mergendoller, J. R. (1993). Introduction: The role of research in the reform of middle grades education. *Elementary School Journal, 93,* 443-446.

Merton, R. K. (1957). *Social theory and social structure.* New York: Free Press.

Messick, S. (1989). Validity. In R. E. Linn (Ed.), *Educational measurement* (3rd ed., pp. 13-103). Washington, DC: American Council on Education and National Council on Measurement in Education.

Meyerson, D. E. (1991). Acknowledging and uncovering ambiguities in cultures. In P. J. Frost, L. F. Moore, M. R. Louis, C. C. Lundberg, & J. Martin (Eds.), *Reframing organizational culture* (pp. 254-270). Newbury Park, CA: Sage.

Midgley, C., Feldlaufer, H., & Eccles, J. (1989). Change in teacher efficacy and student self- and task-related beliefs in mathematics during the transition to junior high school. *Journal of Educational Psychology, 81,* 247-258.

Miles, M. (1969). Planned change and organizational health: Figure and ground. In F. D. Carver & T. J. Sergiovanni (Eds.), *Organizations and human behavior* (pp. 375-391). New York: McGraw-Hill.

Miles, M. B. (1975). Comment from Miles. *Urban Education, 10,* 46-48.

Mintzberg, H. (1983). *Power in and around organizations.* Englewood Cliffs, NJ: Prentice Hall.

Miskel, C., DeFrain, J., & Wilcox, K. (1980). A test of expectancy work motivation theory in educational organizations. *Educational Administration Quarterly, 16,* 70-92.

Miskel, C., Fevurly, R., & Stewart, J. (1979). Organizational structures and processes, perceived school effectiveness, loyalty, and job satisfaction. *Educational Administration Quarterly, 15,* 97-118.

Miskel, C., & Ogawa, R. (1988). Work motivation, job satisfaction, and climate. In N. J. Boyan (Ed.), *Handbook of research on educational administration* (pp. 279-304). New York: Longman.

Moore, W., & Esselman, M. (1992, April). *Teacher efficacy, power, school climate, and achievement: A desegregating district's experience.* Paper presented at the annual meeting of the American Educational Research Association, San Francisco.

Moos, R. (1979). *Evaluating educational environments.* San Francisco: Jossey-Bass.

Moss, P. A. (1992). Validity in educational measurement. *Review of Educational Research, 62,* 229-258.

Mott, P. (1972). *Characteristics of effective organizations.* New York: Harper & Row.

Mowday, R. T., Steers, R. M., & Porter, L. W. (1979). The measurement of organizational commitment. *Journal of Vocational Behavior, 14,* 224-247.

Mullins, J. (1976). *Analysis and synthesis of research utilizing the organizational climate descriptive questionnaire: Organizations other than elementary schools.* Unpublished doctoral dissertation, University of Georgia, Athens.

Murphy, J., Weil, M., Hallinger, P., & Mitman, A. (1982). Academic press: Translating high expectations into school policies and classroom practices. *Educational Leadership, 40,* 22-26.

Ouchi, W. (1981). *Theory Z.* Reading, MA: Addison-Wesley.

Ouchi, W., & Wilkins, A. L. (1985). Organizational culture. *Annual Review of Sociology, 11,* 457-483.

Pace, C. R., & Stern, G. C. (1958). An approach to the measure of psychological characteristics of college environments. *Journal of Educational Psychology, 49,* 269-277.

Pallas, A. M., & Neumann, A. (1993, April). *Blinded by the light: The applicability of total management to educational organizations.* Paper presented at the annual meeting of the American Educational Research Association, Atlanta, GA.

Parsons, T. (1951). *The social system.* Glencoe, IL: Free Press.

Parsons, T. (1961). An outline of the social system. In T. Parsons, E. Shils, K. D. Naegele, & J. R. Pitts (Eds.), *Theories of society: Foundations of modern sociological theory* (Vol. 1, pp. 30-79). New York: Free Press.

Parsons, T. (1967). Some ingredients of a general theory of formal organization. In A. W. Halpin (Ed.), *Administrative theory in education* (pp. 40-72). New York: Macmillan.

Parsons, T., Bales, R. F., & Shils, E. A. (1953). *Working papers in the theory of action.* Glencoe, IL: Free Press.

Pascale, R. T., & Athos, A. (1981). *The art of Japanese management.* New York: Simon & Schuster.

Pelz, D. C. (1952). Influence: A key to effective leadership in the firstline supervisor, *Personnel, 29,* 209-217.

Peters, T., & Waterman, R. (1982). *In search of excellence: Lessons from America's best-run companies.* New York: Harper & Row.

Pettigrew, A. W. (1979). On studying organizational culture. *Administrative Science Quarterly, 24,* 570-581.

Price, J. L., & Mueller, C. W. (1986). *Handbook of organizational measurement.* Marshfield, MA: Pitman.

Purkey, S. C., & Smith, M. S. (1983). Effective schools: A review. *Elementary School Journal, 83,* 427-452.

Radcliffe-Brown, A. (1952). *Structure and function in primitive society.* London, UK: Oxford University Press.

Ralph, J. H., & Fennessey, J. J. (1983). Science or reform: Some questions about the effective schools model. *Phi Delta Kappan, 64,* 689-694.

Rhodes, L. A. (1990). Why quality is within our grasp . . . if we reach. *School Administrator, 47*(10), 31-34.

Riggs, I., & Enochs, L. (1990). Toward the development of an elementary teacher's science teaching efficacy belief instrument. *Science Education, 74,* 625-638.

Rokeach, M. (1960). *The open and closed mind.* New York: Basic Books.

Rose, J. S., & Medway, F. J. (1981). Measurement of teachers' beliefs in their control over student outcome. *Journal of Educational Research 74,* 185-190.

Rosenholtz, S. J. (1985). Political myths about educational reform: Lessons from research on teaching. *Phi Delta Kappan, 65,* 349-355.

Rosenholtz, S. J. (1989). *Teachers' workplace: The social organization of schools.* White Plains, NY: Longman.

Ross, J. A. (1992). Teacher efficacy and the effect of coaching on student achievement. *Canadian Journal of Education, 17,* 51-65.

Ross, J. A., Cousins, J. B., & Gadalla, T. (1996). Within-teacher predictors of teacher efficacy. *Teaching and Teacher Education, 12,* 385-400.

Rotter, J. B. (1967). A new scale for the measure of interpersonal trust. *Journal of Personality, 35,* 651-655.

Rowan, B., Bossert S. T., & Dwyer, D. C. (1983). Research on schools: A cautionary note. *Educational Researcher, 12,* 24-31.

Schein, E. H. (1985). *Organizational culture and leadership.* San Francisco: Jossey-Bass.

Schein, E. H. (1990). Organizational culture. *American Psychologist, 45,* 109-119.

Schein, E. H. (1992). *Organizational culture and leadership* (2nd ed.). San Francisco: Jossey-Bass.

Scherkenbach, W. (1992). *The Deming route to quality and production.* Washington, DC: CEEPress.

Schneider, B. (1990). *Organizational climate and culture.* San Francisco: Jossey-Bass.

Schwandt, D. R. (1978). *Analysis of school organizational climate research 1962-1977: Toward construct clarification.* Unpublished doctoral dissertation, Wayne State University, Detroit, MI.

Schwartz, H. M., & Davis, S. M. (1981) Matching corporate culture and business strategy. *Organizational Dynamics, 10,* 30-48.

Seeman, M. (1966). Status and identity: The problem of authenticity. *Pacific Sociological Review, 9,* 67-73.

Selznick, P. (1957). *Leadership in administration.* New York: Harper & Row.

Senge, P. (1990). *The fifth discipline: The art and practice of the learning organization.* New York: Doubleday.

Sergiovanni, T. J. (1991). *Moral leadership.* San Francisco: Jossey-Bass.

Sergiovanni, T. J. (1992). Moral authority and the regeneration of supervision. In C. D. Glickman (Ed.), *Supervision in transition: The 1992 ASCD yearbook* (pp. 203-214). Alexandria, VA: American Association for Supervision and Curriculum Development.

Shouse, R. C., & Brinson, K. H., Jr. (1995, October). Sense of community and academic effectiveness in American high schools: Some cautionary, yet promising evidence from NELS:88. Paper presented at the annual meeting of the University Council for Educational Administration, Salt Lake City, UT.

Silver, P. (1983). *Educational administration: Theoretical perspectives in practice and research.* New York: Harper & Row.

Sirotnik, K. A. (1980). Psychometric implications of the unit-of-analysis problem (with examples from the measurement of organizational climate). *Journal of Educational Measurement, 17,* 245-282.

Slavin, R. E. (1991). Synthesis on research on cooperative learning. *Educational Leadership, 48*(5), 71-82.

Smylie, M. A. (1988). The enhancement function of staff development: organizational and psychological antecedents to individual teacher change. *American Educational Research Journal, 25,* 1-30.

Stern, G. G. (1970). *People in context: Measuring person-environment in education and industry.* New York: John Wiley.

Taguiri, R. (1968). The concept of organizational climate. In R. Taguiri & G. W. Litwin (Eds.), *Organizational climate: Explorations of a concept* (pp. 1-32). Boston: Harvard University, Division of Research, Graduate School of Business Administration.

Tarter, C. J., Bliss, J. R., & Hoy, W. K. (1989). School characteristics and faculty trust in secondary schools. *Educational Administration Quarterly, 25, 3,* 294-308.

Tarter, C. J., & Hoy, W. K. (1988). The context of trust: Teachers and the principal. *High School Journal, 72,* 17-22.

Tarter, C. J., Sabo, D., & Hoy, W. K. (1995). Middle school climate, faculty trust, and effectiveness: A path analysis. *Journal of Research and Development in Education, 29,* 41-49.

Toepfer, C. F. (1990). Middle-level school grades and program development. In *Schools in the middle: A report on trends and practices* (pp. 37-58). Reston, VA: National Association of Secondary School Principals.

Tracs, S., & Gibson, S. (1986, November). *Effects of efficacy on academic achievement.* Paper presented at the annual meeting of the California Educational Research Association, Marina del Rey, CA.

Trentham, L., Silvern, S. B., & Brogdon, R. (1985). Teacher efficacy and teacher competency ratings. *Psychology in Schools, 22,* 343-352.

Watkins, J. F. (1968). The OCDQ—An application and some implications. *Educational Administration Quarterly, 4,* 46-61.

Wax, A., & Dutton, M. (1991, April). *The relationship between teacher use of cooperative learning and efficacy.* Paper presented at the annual meeting of the American Educational Research Association, Chicago.

Woolfolk, A. E., Rosoff, B., & Hoy, W. K. (1990). Prospective teachers' sense of efficacy and their beliefs about managing students. *Teaching and Teacher Education, 6,* 137-148.

INDEX

CORWIN
PRESS

The Corwin Press logo—a raven striding across an open book—
represents the happy union of courage and learning. We are a
professional-level publisher of books and journals for K–12
educators, and we are committed to creating and providing resources that embody these qualities. Corwin's motto is "Success for All
Learners."